# Grammar Rules!

Tanya Gibb

NSW Edition

Name: ____________________

Class: ____________________

**Grammar Rules! Student Book 3**
**NSW Edition**
**ISBN: 978 0 6550 9243 8**

Designer and typesetter: Trish Hayes
Illustrator: Stephen Michael King
Series editor: Marie James
Indigenous consultant: Al Fricker

**Acknowledgement of Country**
We acknowledge the Aboriginal and Torres Strait Islander peoples of this nation. We acknowledge the Traditional Custodians on whose unceded lands we have created this resource. We pay our respects to ancestors and Elders past and present.

This edition published in 2024 by **Matilda Education Australia**, an imprint of Meanwhile Education Pty
Melbourne, Australia
T: 1300 277 235
E: customersupport@matildaed.com.au
W: www.matildaeducation.com.au

First edition published in 2008 by Macmillan Science and Education Australia Pty Ltd


**Publication data**
Author: Tanya Gibb
Title: *Grammar Rules! Student Book 3 NSW Edition*
ISBN: 978 0 6550 9243 8

A catalogue record for this book is available from the National Library of Australia

Printed in China by Central
Jun-2025

# Contents

# NOTE TO TEACHERS AND PARENTS

## Grammar Rules!

*Grammar Rules!* comprehensively meets the requirements of the 2022 NSW Education Standards Authority **English K–10 Syllabus Rationale**, which recognises that knowledge, skills, values and attitudes acquired in English enable students to become 'confident communicators, critical and imaginative thinkers, lifelong learners and informed, active participants in Australian society.'

Learning in English is recursive and accumulative, so each student workbook in the *Grammar Rules!* series is designed to build on the concepts covered previously and for an expanding range of purposes and audiences.

*Grammar Rules!* provides a conceptually sound, scope and sequence of context-based activities that support teaching and learning in English. Although the title for the series is *Grammar Rules!*, the series in not just about grammar. Each unit of work in the series begins at the level of the whole text by identifying purpose and audience for the model text, providing teaching opportunities to activate students' background knowledge of the topic or the text type, and then supporting students in reading comprehension. The texts provided can be used for discussion of text forms and features and sentence structures, as well as for vocabulary expansion. The texts can also be used as models for students to use when creating their own written, spoken or multimodal texts. The texts included in *Grammar Rules!* cover a variety of informative, imaginative and persuasive texts and hybrid texts that use elements of different types of texts.

*Grammar Rules!* also teaches the conventions of punctuation and some aspects of spelling (for example, plural nouns, suffixes and prefixes); literary elements such as onomatopoeia, rhyme and alliteration; and the way visual elements function to support or construct meaning. Other areas of the **English K–10 Syllabus** covered in *Grammar Rules!* include critical reading and reflecting on character, setting and plot in narrative texts (literature).

## Student Book 3

### Units of work

*Student Book 3* contains 35 weekly units of work presented in a conceptually sound scope and sequence. The intention is for students to work through the units in the sequence in which they are presented. See the **Scope and Sequence Chart** on pages 6–7 for more information. There are regular Revision Units that can be used for consolidation or assessment purposes.

The sample texts in *Student Book 3* are not tied to any particular content across other curriculum areas, but are generally based on the theme of inventions and discoveries. This allows teachers and students to focus on the way language is structured in the different types of texts according to purpose and audience. Students can then use this knowledge to critically evaluate, respond to and create texts in other learning areas.

### Icons

Encourages students to create texts of their own to demonstrate their understanding of the text structures and features taught in the unit. These activities focus on written language; however, many also provide opportunities for using spoken language to engage with others, make presentations and develop skills in using ICT resources.

Highlights useful grammatical rules and concepts. The rule is always introduced the first time students need it to complete an activity.

Tells students that a special hint is provided for an activity. It might be a tip about language features, or a reminder to look at a rule in a previous unit.

### Grammar Rules! Glossary

A valuable glossary is provided at the end of *Student Book 3*. Teachers and students can use this as a reference for terminology and rules covered in *Student Book 3*. Page references are also given for the point in the book where the rule was first introduced, so that students can go back to that unit if they need more information or further revision of the concept.

## Pull-Out Writing Log

At the centre of *Student Book 3* is a practical pull-out Writing Log so that students can keep track of the texts they have created or attempted to create. The Writing Log also includes a handy reminder of the writing process, as well as a checklist of types of texts for students to try.

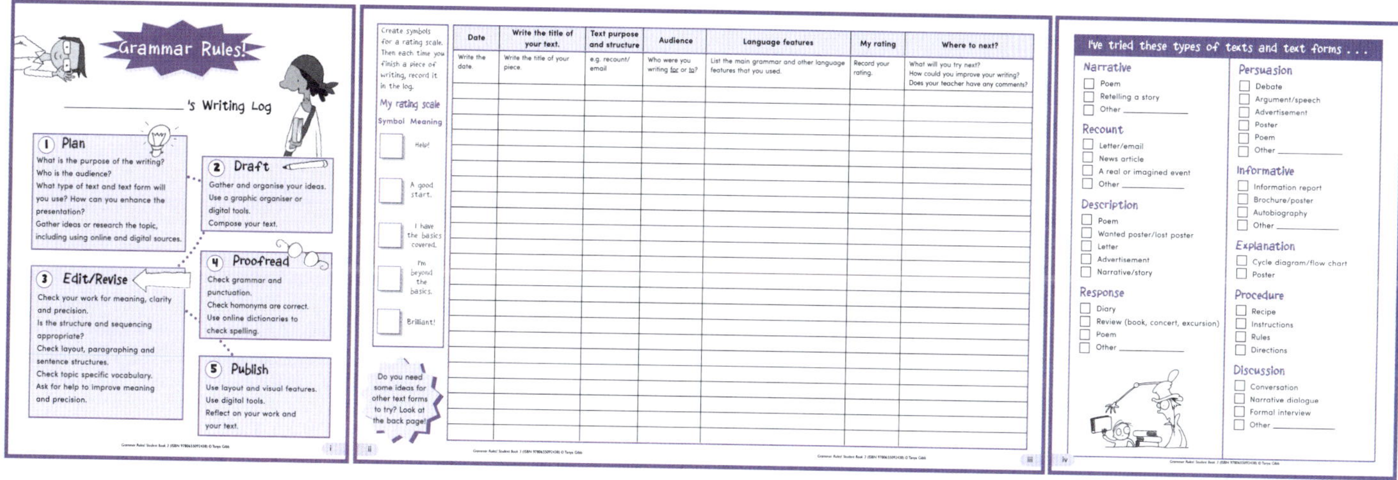


## Unit At A Glance

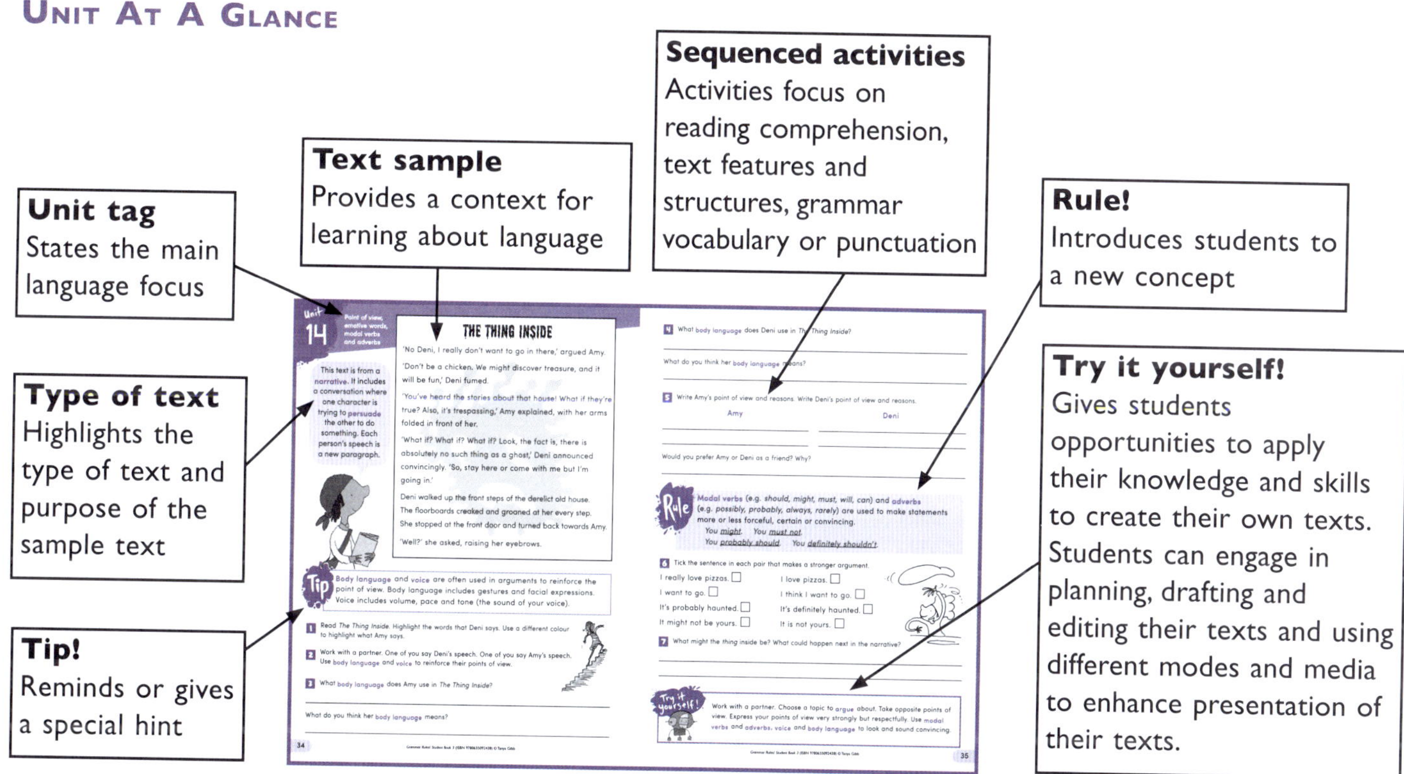


## Grammar Rules! Teacher Resource Book 3–6

Full teacher support for *Student Book 3* is provided by *Grammar Rules! Teacher Resource Book 3–6*. Here you will find valuable background information about teaching English along with practical resources, such as:

- strategies for teaching text structures and features
- literacy games and activities
- assessment strategies.
- grammar and punctuation wall charts
- teaching tips for every unit in *Student Book 3*
- answers for every unit in *Student Book 3*

## Scope and Sequence

This scope and sequence chart is based on the requirements of the NSW English K–10 Syllabus.

| Unit | Unit name<br>Type of text | Purpose of text | Clauses, sentences, connectives, conjunctions | Nouns, noun groups, pronouns, adjectives | Verbs and verb groups | Adverbs and adverbial phrases | Elements of language |
|---|---|---|---|---|---|---|---|
| 1 | **Museum Visit**<br>Personal recount | to retell events<br>to respond | | proper and common nouns | action verbs, past tense | | |
| 2 | **My Grandparents**<br>Response | to inform<br>to describe | clauses, simple sentences | adjectives, proper and common nouns | | | definitions, sentence boundary punctuation |
| 3 | **Dear Nana and Pop**<br>Email | to respond | sentences, questions, exclamations | personal pronouns | thinking and feeling verbs | | sentence boundary punctuation |
| 4 | **The Case of the Missing Robots**<br>Narrative | to entertain | | personal pronouns, noun groups, articles, adjectives | | | character, setting, mystery genre |
| 5 | **Inventing Potato Chips**<br>Film review | to respond<br>to persuade | | | saying verbs, thinking verbs | | opinions |
| 6 | REVISION | | | | | | |
| 7 | **My Special Place**<br>Poem | to respond<br>to describe | | noun groups, adjectives | | adverbials that tell where | |
| 8 | **Use Less Plastic!**<br>Speech<br>Argument | to persuade<br>to argue a point of view | | possessive apostrophes | | | main idea, apostrophes for contractions, opinion and reasons |
| 9 | **Penicillin**<br>Information report | to inform | questions and statements | | relating (being) verbs | adverbs/ phrases for time (adverbials) | sequencing events in time |
| 10 | **Molly's Discovery**<br>Narrative | to entertain | independent clauses, compound sentences, conjunctions | singular and plural nouns | subject-verb agreement | | character, setting, suffixes for plurals |
| 11 | **Search for the Lost Valley**<br>Narrative | to entertain | exclamations | adjectives | | adverbs that tell how | onomatopoeia, character, setting |
| 12 | REVISION | | | | | | |
| 13 | **Trampolines**<br>Discussion<br>Conversation | to share opinions | quoted speech, questions and statements | adjectives | saying verbs | adverbs | opinions, evaluative language |
| 14 | **The Thing Inside**<br>Narrative<br>Discussion | to argue a point of view | | | modal verbs, saying verbs | modal adverbs | body language, voice, characters' dialogue |
| 15 | **Jane Goodall**<br>Biography | to inform | sentences | possessive pronouns | | | word families, commas in a list and for quoted speech |
| 16 | **Wiz Bang 3000 Kitchen Hand!**<br>Advertisement | to persuade | commands | personal pronouns | modal verbs | modal adverbs | emotive words |
| 17 | **Bush Tucker**<br>Information report | to inform<br>to respond<br>to describe | | noun groups, articles, adjectives that compare | | | |
| 18 | REVISION | | | | | | |


*Grammar Rules! Student Book 3* (ISBN 9780655092438) © Tanya Gibb

| Unit | Unit name<br>Type of text | Purpose of text | Clauses, sentences, connectives, conjunctions | Nouns, noun groups, pronouns, adjectives | Verbs and verb groups | Adverbs and adverbial phrases | Elements of language |
|---|---|---|---|---|---|---|---|
| 19 | **Haiku**<br>Information report | to inform<br>to describe | | adjectives | | adverbials | imagery, idiom, simile |
| 20 | **Recycle!**<br>Speech<br>Argument | to persuade | sentences, connectives | | | | evaluative language, fact/opinion |
| 21 | **Professor Snodgrass Fails Again**<br>Narrative – comic strip | to entertain | quoted speech | | | | speech balloons, stereotypes, character |
| 22 | **Dinosaur Found at Local School**<br>News report | to inform<br>to report newsworthy events | quoted speech | adjectives, abstract nouns | modal verbs | adverbs | emotive words, synonyms, sensationalism |
| 23 | **The Discovery**<br>Narrative | to entertain | | adjectives | verbs, past, present and future tense | | story character, judging a character, narrative voice |
| 24 | REVISION | | | | | | |
| 25 | **The Best New Invention**<br>Discussion – conversation | to persuade | conjunctions, complex sentences | | modal verbs | modal adverbs | paragraphs |
| 26 | **Creation Stories**<br>Information report | to inform | | noun groups, adjectives – describing and number/quantity | | | prefixes, suffixes, punctuation |
| 27 | **Warts, Festers and Carbuncle Remover**<br>Recipe | to inform<br>to instruct | commands | adjectives | action verbs | adverbs | definitions |
| 28 | **How the Alarm Bed Works**<br>Explanation | to explain<br>to inform | conjunctions | | verb groups | adverbs | sequencing information |
| 29 | **How to Use the Drolley (or Dog Trolley)**<br>Instructions | to instruct<br>to inform | sentences, clauses, commands | noun groups, classifying adjectives | | | logical order |
| 30 | REVISION | | | | | | |
| 31 | **My Home**<br>Poem | to respond<br>to inform<br>to persuade | | personal pronouns, collective nouns | subject-verb agreement | | main idea, point of view, narrator |
| 32 | **Can We Negotiate?**<br>Discussion<br>Conversation | to present opinions<br>to persuade | sentences – statements, questions, commands, exclamations | | saying verbs | | antonyms, synonyms, punctuation, point of view |
| 33 | **Clever Inventions**<br>Information report | to inform<br>to persuade | abstract nouns | personal pronouns | modal verbs, verb groups | | punctuation |
| 34 | **The Invention of Money**<br>Information report | to inform | | personal pronouns, noun groups | | | homophones, commas in lists, homonyms |
| 35 | REVISION | | | | | | |

Unit 1

Nouns, action verbs, tense

# Museum Visit

On the weekend, Mum took me to the National Museum of Australia in Canberra.

We saw lots of interesting exhibits and displays. My favourite was the Aboriginal language game. I had to match words in the Guugu Yimithirr language with words listed by James Cook's crew on *Endeavour* in 1770. I found out that 'kangaroo' is a Guugu Yimithirr word.

We ate lunch beside Lake Burley Griffin and then we saw Paddle Steamer *Enterprise*. It is one of the oldest working paddle steamers in the world.

I had a great day.

Rule

**Nouns** name people, places, animals and things, including ideas.
Common nouns: *teachers* *museum* *cockatoo* *book* *peace*
**Proper nouns** are particular names. They begin with a capital letter.
*First Nations Australians* *Hobart* *Tasmanian devil* *Monday*

**1** Read *Museum Visit*. Write six **common nouns** used in *Museum Visit*.

---

**2** Write six **proper nouns** used in *Museum Visit*.

---

Book and text titles and names of organisations begin with a capital letter.
*'The Emu Who Ran Through the Sky' by Helen Milroy, published by Magabala Books.*

**3** Write the title of your favourite book or television show. Use capital letters.

---



*Grammar Rules! Student Book 3* (ISBN 9780655092438) © Tanya Gibb

**4** Underline six **nouns** for people, places, animals or things.

We parked our car under a tree.

We watched a film about bees.

We sat at a table to eat.

Many people visit the museum.

**5** Circle the **noun** in each row.

| | | | |
|---|---|---|---|
| dog | skipped | ate | played |
| visited | drove | saw | cat |
| stopped | bird | climbed | watched |
| jumped | tickled | swan | said |
| talked | sang | wiggled | wombat |

**Verbs** tell what is happening in a clause. Verbs anchor events in time. This is called **tense**. Past tense verbs show that activities happened in the past.

**Past tense action verbs:** *jumped ran made wrote ate had eaten*

**6** Underline an **action verb** in each sentence.

We ate lunch.

Mum drove the car.

We walked beside the lake.

I built a robot.

We arrived at 10 o'clock.

**7** Write the **past tense** form for each **action verb**.

skip ______________

break ______________

see ______________

know ______________

teach ______________

**8** Choose an **action verb** from the box to complete each sentence.

| visited | worked | slept | swam |
|---|---|---|---|

We ______________ the museum.

Ducks ______________ on the lake.

I ______________ well after my big day.

Dad ______________ all day.

Write a **response** to somewhere you have been or something you have seen. Make sure you tell who, what, when and where. Read your text to others in the class. Adjust the **volume**, **pitch** and **pace** of your reading to keep listeners interested. Use eye contact.

Unit 2 Adjectives, clauses

This text is **informative**. The writer tells about their grandparents.

# My Grandparents

In 1977, my grandparents came to live in Australia. They were refugees from Vietnam.

When they arrived in Australia, my grandparents had no possessions and they did not speak English. Life was difficult at first, but they were very brave and they worked hard.

My family is proud of our Vietnamese heritage. Our most important celebration is Tết, or New Year. At Tết, we clean the house and we get new clothes and eat special foods. My grandparents, parents and uncle give me 'lucky money'.

I love Tết and I love my grandparents.

**Rule** An **adjective** tells more about a noun. An adjective can describe.
*Tết is my favourite celebration. It is fun.*

**1** Use **adjectives** from *My Grandparents* to complete the sentences.

Vietnamese New Year is ____________ to the writer's family.

The writer's grandparents were ____________ to come to a new country.

New Year is celebrated with ____________ clothes and ____________ foods.

The writer loves ____________ money.

The grandparents worked ____________.

Life in Australia was ____________ at first.

**2** An explorer is a person who sets out to discover new or unfamiliar areas. Would you call the writer's grandparents explorers? Explain.

______________________________________________

______________________________________________

**3** Underline the **proper nouns** in *My Grandparents*.



*Grammar Rules! Student Book 3* (ISBN 9780655092438) © Tanya Gibb

**4** List all the **common nouns** used for people in *My Grandparents.*

______________________________________________

______________________________________________

**5** Write a definition for *refugee*. Use a dictionary.

______________________________________________

**Rule**

A **clause** is a unit of meaning that includes a **verb**. A single clause is a **simple sentence**. Sentences begin with a capital letter and end with a full stop, question mark or exclamation mark.

*Today is Friday.* *Are you busy?* *Stop that!*

**6** Underline each group of words that is a **sentence**. Add a full stop, question mark or exclamation mark for each sentence.

Hard-working grandparents

The dog ate my homework

Bronte and Lee

Will Mum make spring rolls

Dad told me which

**7** Unscramble each **sentence**. Rewrite it correctly with **punctuation** marks.

australia mum was born in

______________________________________________

can vietnam we visit

______________________________________________

the finish line run to quickly

______________________________________________

celebrations new year are fun vietnamese

______________________________________________

Interview a family member. Find out about your family history or a particular celebration your family enjoys. Create a multimodal text to share information about your family with your class.

Unit 3

## Personal pronouns, thinking and feeling verbs

This email is a **response** that gives the writer's point of view. It uses **personal pronouns**.

Dear Nana and Pop,

I am excited for the next school holidays. Jack says we will drive up there on the Saturday morning.

I hope Shadow remembers me!

Yesterday, Dad told me that archaeologists have discovered cave art in Australia that was painted 170 000 years ago. I think that is incredible. The discovery means that First Nations Australians lived in Australia much earlier than people knew about.

I miss you.

I LOVE YOU, Hannah

**Rule**

**Personal pronouns** are words that refer to or replace **nouns**. They help track a person or thing across a text.

*I me we us you he she her him they them it*

*The dingo ran away because she was frightened.*

**1** Read *Dear Nana and Pop*. Circle the **personal pronouns**.

**2** Write a **personal pronoun** from the box on each line. Circle other personal pronouns in the sentences.

| He | me | it | They | She | them | It | you |
|---|---|---|---|---|---|---|---|

Will and Kyle are coming on Saturday. __________ are looking forward to it.

Pass the scissors to Gemma. __________ needs __________.

Follow Harry. __________ will show you the way.

A magpie swooped me today. __________ scared __________.

Can I have a mango? I'll share __________ with __________.

**Thinking** and **feeling verbs** are verbs for thoughts and feelings.

*feel think hope wondered remembered loved*

**3** Find and underline the **thinking** and **feeling verbs** in *Dear Nana and Pop.*

**4** Circle the **thinking** or **feeling verb** in each simple sentence.

I hope Nana and Pop visit us soon.

I forgot my library book today.

I like banana cake best.

I remembered my homework.

Brett decided that he likes broccoli after all.

**5** In *Dear Nana and Pop,* where is Jack taking Hannah in the next school holidays?

______________________________________________

**6** Write a **sentence** to answer each question.

How old are you?

______________________________________________

Who lives with you?

______________________________________________

What is your favourite food?

______________________________________________

**7** Find a sentence that is an exclamation in *Dear Nana and Pop.* Copy it onto the line.

______________________________________________

Write a letter or an email to a friend or relative. Tell them about something that you are excited about. Use **thinking** and **feeling verbs** and **personal pronouns**. Take care to punctuate your sentences correctly.

Unit 4

Personal pronouns, noun groups, articles

This text is the beginning of a **mystery narrative**. It uses **noun groups** to describe the setting and main character.

# The Case of the Missing Robots

On a peaceful island off the coast of Australia, there lived a clever inventor. The inventor made robots with artificial intelligence. This meant they could think for themselves.

The inventor lived alone. He had no human friends, only the robots, and he loved them.

One day, there was a huge explosion outside the robot factory. The inventor went inside to check on his robots, but he couldn't find a single one. They had completely disappeared.

**1** Read *The Case of the Missing Robots*. What might the rest of the story be about?

______________________________________________

**2** Read *The Case of the Missing Robots*. Circle the **personal pronouns**.

What **noun** does *He/he* refer to? ____________

What **noun** do *they* and *them* refer to? ____________

**3** Complete each sentence using a **personal pronoun** from the box.
Use a capital letter if the **pronoun** begins a sentence.

| he | she | they | them |
|---|---|---|---|

____________ went to find his robots. He couldn't find ____________.

____________ were missing. The worried inventor phoned his mother.

____________ told him not to worry.



*Grammar Rules! Student Book 3* (ISBN 9780655092438) © Tanya Gibb

**4** Complete each sentence. Use the **personal pronouns** from the box. Use a capital letter if the pronoun begins a sentence.

| it | it | it | he | them | they |
|---|---|---|---|---|---|

The island is off the coast. __________ is a beautiful place.

The inventor builds robots. __________ invents __________.

A fast boat collects the robots. __________ arrives each month.

The explosion was outside the factory. __________ was very loud.

The robots had vanished. __________ were nowhere to be seen.

**Rule**

A **noun group** is a group of words that includes a **noun**. A noun group can begin with an **article** (*a, an, the*). A noun group can include **adjectives** that describe (*the missing robots*) or tell number or quantity (*two robots, a few years*).

**5** Underline four **adjectives** in *The Case of the Missing Robots*.

**6** Add a **noun** from *The Case of the Missing Robots* to form **noun groups**.

clever __________

peaceful __________

huge __________

artificial __________

**7** Draw lines to link each **adjective** to a **noun**.

| | |
|---|---|
| happy | ghost |
| angry | pirate |
| scary | smile |
| ferocious | voice |
| whiny | frown |

**8** Add an **article** and an interesting **adjective** of your own to form **noun groups**.

__________ spaceship

__________ discovery

__________ experiment

__________ journey

__________ scientist

__________ alien

**Try it yourself!**

Finish the **narrative** *The Case of the Missing Robots*. Why had the robots disappeared? What will the inventor do? How will the story end? Ask a classmate to help you revise your draft before publishing and sharing it with others in the class.

Unit 5

Saying and thinking verbs, opinions

# Inventing Potato Chips

I saw a really entertaining movie about the invention of potato chips. A chef in a restaurant in America, in about 1850, made French fries. A customer complained that the fries weren't thin enough. The chef made them thinner and thinner, but the customer said they still weren't thin enough. Finally, the chef fried paper-thin slices and sprinkled them with plenty of salt. The customer said they were fantastic. So that's how potato chips were invented. The movie was very funny. I enjoyed it and I think you would enjoy it too.

This film review is a persuasive text. It is a **response** to a movie. It includes the writer's **opinion**.

**Rule**

**Saying verbs** are verbs that show you something has been said.

*asked* *screamed* *shouted*

**1** Read *Inventing Potato Chips*. Underline the **saying verbs**.

**2** Write a **saying verb** of your own on the line.

'These chips are fantastic!' ________________ the happy customer.

**3** Use a **saying verb** from the box to complete each sentence.

| stated | cheered | told | asked | announced |
|---|---|---|---|---|

The customer ________________ that the fries were too thick.

The customer ________________ the chef to try again.

The customer ________________ the chef to make the fries thinner.

The customer ________________ the fries were perfect.

The chef ________________ when the customer was happy.



*Grammar Rules! Student Book 3* (ISBN 9780655092438) © Tanya Gibb

**4** Write a sentence for each **saying verb** in the box.

| whispered<br>yelled<br>cried |
|---|

______________________________

______________________________

______________________________

**Tip** Film and book reviews use **thinking** and **feeling verbs** to express opinions.

**5** Write the sentence from *Inventing Potato Chips* that uses a **thinking** or **feeling verb** to tell you the writer's opinion.

______________________________

**6** Finish the sentence.

The writer said the movie was ______________________________.

**7** Write *fact* or *opinion* after each sentence.

I loved the movie. ____________

Potato chips are healthy. ____________

Potato chips are made from potatoes. ____________

Chefs must be clever at inventing new recipes. ____________

Everyone loves potato chips. ____________

**8** Write a **fact** about your class.

______________________________

______________________________

______________________________

**9** Write an **opinion** about your class.

______________________________

______________________________

______________________________

Write a review of a movie, book or television show that you have enjoyed or a song you like. Write your opinions about it. Use **thinking** and **feeling verbs** and **adjectives**.

# Revision

**1** Rewrite each sentence with correct punctuation.

aunty flo lives in darwin

______________________________

today is wednesday

______________________________

school holidays begin in april

______________________________

**2** Write eight **common nouns** for things in your classroom.

______________________________

______________________________

**3** Underline the **action verbs** in the box.

| jumped | house | science | island | invented | cooked |
|---|---|---|---|---|---|

**4** Write a **sentence** telling what each animal did.

______________________________ ______________________________

______________________________ ______________________________

______________________________ ______________________________

**5** Unscramble each **thinking** or **feeling verb**.

ovedl ____________ tedha ____________ beedliev ____________

pohed ____________ shiwde ____________ eedend ____________



*Grammar Rules! Student Book 3* (ISBN 9780655092438) © Tanya Gibb

**6** Complete each sentence with a **personal pronoun** from the box. Use a capital letter if the pronoun begins a sentence.

| we | us | they | them |
|---|---|---|---|

Give ________ their books.

________ can come with us.

________ enjoy watching movies together.

Will you watch the movie with ________?

**7** Unjumble the words and write the **sentences**. Use correct punctuation.

potato tasty I think chips are

______________________________________________

pancakes I love for breakfast to eat

______________________________________________

going you the are to watch movie

______________________________________________

away go

______________________________________________

**8** Form **noun groups**. Draw a line to link an **adjective** to each **noun**.

| | |
|---|---|
| cute | island |
| sore | king |
| bossy | dog |
| old | knee |
| beautiful | kitten |

**9** Write *fact* or *opinion* after each sentence.

Computers are machines. ____________

All sharks are scary. ____________

I love broccoli. ____________

Magpies are birds. ____________

**10** Complete each sentence with a **saying verb**.

The mother ______________ to her baby.

The scientist ______________ everyone about her discovery.

The chef ______________ with the customer.

Team members ______________ when they won.

Unit 7

Adverbials, adjectives

The poet uses **prepositional phrases** with **adjectives** to tell where.

# My Special Place

My special place
at the bottom of the yard,
under scraggy bushes,
through prickly hedges,
into a dark tunnel,
beneath the overgrowth –
still and quiet.
Secret place –
discovered and hidden.

**Rule**

**Adverbials** tell where, when or how. Some adverbials are phrases that begin with a preposition. These can also be called **prepositional phrases**.

*beside the creek*   *at 5 o'clock*   *over it*   *with Oly*

**1** Read *My Special Place*. Circle the **adverbials** that tell where.

**2** Use a word from the box to make **phrases** in each **sentence**.

| over | under | behind | through | on |
|---|---|---|---|---|

Jump ______________ the fence.

Look ______________ the rug.

Crawl ______________ the tunnel.

Sit ______________ the log.

Hide it ______________ your back.

**3** Circle all the words that could be used in this sentence.

I crawled ____________ the branch.

| over | through | into | beside | from | around | above | along |
|---|---|---|---|---|---|---|---|



*Grammar Rules! Student Book 3* (ISBN 9780655092438) © Tanya Gibb

**4** Circle all the words that could be used in this sentence.

I looked __________ the fence.

| during | near | towards | under | around | without | before | beyond |
|---|---|---|---|---|---|---|---|

**5** Write **adverbials** that tell where or when to complete the sentences.

Let's go to the park ______________________________.

We'll eat the popcorn ______________________________.

Brush your teeth ______________________________.

The movie starts ______________________________.

**6** Complete each sentence with an **adverbial** to tell where.

The lorikeets chattered ______________________________.

The dog squeezed ______________________________.

The tiger prowled ______________________________.

The worms wriggled ______________________________.

**7** Underline the **adjectives** in *My Special Place.*

**8** Write new **adjectives** to give a different description of the special place.

Tip: Remember the rule on page 10.

under ______________ bushes

through ______________ hedges

into a ______________ tunnel

**9** Write two **adjectives** to describe each **noun**.

______________ ______________ apple

______________ ______________ bedroom

______________ ______________ mango

______________ ______________ hamburger

**Try it yourself!**

Write a **poem** about a special place where you like to go. It could be a cubbyhouse, your local park or somewhere in your home. Use **adverbials** to tell where. Use interesting **adjectives** to describe your special place.

Unit 8

Main idea, contractions, possessive apostrophes

# Use Less Plastic!

Plastic is a very useful invention, but it has become a huge problem in the environment.

Plastic doesn't rot and decompose to feed the earth like plant and animal matter. Large pieces of plastic choke animals or the animals get entangled in it and die. In the environment, plastic breaks down into smaller and smaller pieces that we can't see. These tiny pieces are in the air, in dirt and dust, in our water and our oceans, in our food and even in us.

Plastic can be recycled but most of it isn't. It just ends up as pollution and plastic lasts forever. People should use less plastic!

**Rule** The **main idea** in a text is the idea the author wants you to accept or believe.

**1** What is the **main idea** in *Use Less Plastic!*? To identify the main idea ask: What is it that the author wants me to accept?

______________________________________________

**2** What reasons does the author of *Use Less Plastic!* give to support the **main idea**?

______________________________________________

______________________________________________

**3** Write six **adverbials** that tell <u>where</u> in *Use Less Plastic!*.

______________________________________________

______________________________________________

**4** Find two **adjectives** in *Use Less Plastic!* that are opposite in meaning.

______________________________________________

**5** Find **adjectives** in *Use Less Plastic!* to complete the **noun groups**.

Plastic is a very ______________ invention but also a ______________ problem.

Rule

**Apostrophes** are used in **contractions** to show that letters have been left out.

*do not → don't*   *it is → it's*   *I am → I'm*

**6** Write three **contractions** used in *Use Less Plastic!*. Then write them in their full forms.

____________________   ____________________   ____________________

____________________   ____________________   ____________________

**7** Choose the correct **contraction** from the box. Write it on the line.

| She's It's I'll You'll |
|---|

________ (You will) love the concert.

________ (It is) a Yellow Monday cicada.

________ (I will) help you.

________ (She is) coming by train.

**8** Draw a line to link each **contraction** to the full words.

| | |
|---|---|
| can't | will not |
| shouldn't | cannot |
| aren't | should not |
| won't | did not |
| didn't | are not |

Rule

**Apostrophes** are used to show possession.

For singular nouns use *'s*: *Jed's book, Ella's hat.*

For plural nouns use *s'*: *the teachers own the cars → the teachers' cars.*

If the noun ends in *s* you don't need to add another *s*. *Tess' dog* or *Tess's dog.*

**9** Write the noun on each line to show **possession**. Use an **apostrophe**.

Shalesh lives there. That's ______________ house.

Many dogs were barking. The ______________ barking annoyed us.

Ross owns that ball. That's ______________ ball.

Create a **persuasive** text. What is the **main idea** you want your readers/listeners to accept? What reasons or evidence will you use to support your main idea? Present your text to your class.

Unit 9

Statements, questions, relating verbs, adverbs

# Penicillin

In 1928, a Scottish scientist named Alexander Fleming was studying bacteria growth. Bacteria are germs that can cause infections in people. Fleming discovered that a mould had grown on one of his dishes and that bacteria could not grow where there was mould. He wrote a report about his discovery.

Later, Dr Howard Florey, an Australian, developed penicillin as a medical treatment to kill bacteria. Since then, penicillin has saved millions of lives.

In 1945, Howard Florey, Ernst Chain and Alexander Fleming received the Nobel Peace Prize for Medicine for their work with penicillin.

This **informative** text tells events in a time sequence.

**Rule**

A **statement** gives information or an opinion. It ends in a full stop.
*Marie Curie was a scientist.* *I think Marie Curie was brilliant.*

A **question** asks for information or an opinion. It ends in a question mark.
*What is penicillin?* *Do you think germs are dangerous?*

**1** Read *Penicillin*. Write a **statement** to answer each **question**.

When was Alexander Fleming studying bacteria growth?

_______________________________________________

What are bacteria?

_______________________________________________

Who discovered penicillin?

_______________________________________________

Where was Howard Florey from?

_______________________________________________

How does penicillin work?

_______________________________________________

**2** Write a **question** for each answer.

______________________________ ______________________________

______________________________ ______________________________

**Relating (being) verbs** show relationships, such as being and having. You cannot see any action taking place. *is are have has had was*

**3** Add a **relating verb** from the box to each sentence.

| was<br>is<br>are<br>has<br>had |
|---|

Bacteria __________ germs.

Marie Curie __________ a scientist a long time ago.

What __________ penicillin?

Dillon __________ an allergy to penicillin.

Annie __________ penicillin last month for an infection.

**4** Find three phrases in *Penicillin* that show **time** or sequence.

____________________ ____________________ ____________________

**Adverbs** can **sequence** events in time and tell when.

*then now yesterday soon later always often rarely*

**5** Use a **time word** from the box to complete each sentence.

| soon<br>now<br>later<br>tomorrow |
|---|

The alarm clock will go off __________________.

Shall we go __________________?

I'll show you __________________.

The expedition leaves __________________.

Choose an event from the past that interests you. Write **questions** that you have about the event. Research the event and write a report. Sequence information in time order.

Unit **10** Conjunctions, singular and plural nouns, suffixes

This text is the **orientation** for a **narrative**. It uses **noun groups** for the characters and the setting.

# Molly's Discovery

The sand squished between Oliver's toes. He was playing fetch with his dog, Molly, at the beach. It was a hot day. The beach was crowded, so Oliver and Molly went farther along the beach than usual. They went farther than they had ever ventured before, to the northern end, where nobody ever went. Oliver threw the ball, but when Molly returned, the ball was not in her mouth. In her mouth was a small casket. Molly dropped it at Oliver's feet. Oliver bent down for a closer look. He picked it up and he dusted off the sand. He lifted the lid.

**Rule** **Conjunctions** are words that link words, phrases and clauses in sentences (*and, so, because, or, but*). Two **independent clauses** linked by a conjunction form a **compound sentence**. *I like carrot cake but I prefer banana cake.*

**1** Read *Molly's Discovery*. Circle the compound sentence that uses the **conjunction** *and*.

**2** Use a **conjunction** to join each pair of simple sentences. Write the new sentences on the lines.

Oliver took Molly to the beach. She likes to swim.

____________________________________________

Oliver threw the ball. Molly did not fetch it.

____________________________________________

Molly took off down the beach. Oliver ran after her.

____________________________________________

Molly dropped the casket in the sand. Oliver dusted it off.

____________________________________________

**3** Use the **conjunctions** from the box to join the **clauses** in the sentences.

| because<br>but<br>or |
|---|

Give it back ____________ I will be upset with you.

Give it back ____________ I want a turn.

You can have a turn ____________ I want another turn.

A **noun** can be **singular** or **plural**.

*dog→dogs* *beach→beaches* *mouse→mice* *person→people*

Note that words ending in *y* change *y* to *i* to add *-es* *berry→berries*

Some nouns don't change at all from singular to plural. *fish* *sheep*

**4** Write the **plural** of each **singular noun**.

crowd ______________ adventure ______________ beach ______________

box ______________ battery ______________ city ______________

toe ______________ casket ______________ mouth ______________

**5** Write the **singular** of each **plural noun**.

people ______________ feet ______________ men ______________

women ______________ leaves ______________ lollies ______________

**6** What can you tell about the relationship between Molly and Oliver in *Molly's Discovery*? Explain.

______________________________________________

______________________________________________

In a clause, the **verb** needs to agree with the **subject**.

*The dog plays.* *The dogs play.*

*The dog was running.* *The dogs were running.*

**7** Cross out the incorrect **verb** in each sentence.

Abby (run/runs) faster than her brother.

The boys (swims/swim) very quickly.

The children (eat/eats) lunch at midday.

What will Oliver find in the casket? Finish the **narrative**. Vary the lengths of your sentences to build descriptions or to add suspense. You could create a storyboard for a film of the narrative.

Unit 11

Exclamations, adverbs, onomatopoeia

This text is an **orientation** for a **narrative**. It introduces the main character and the setting. **Adverbs, adjectives** and **onomatopoeia** help to make the story interesting.

# Search for the Lost Valley

Crack! Snap! Alex carelessly stomped over the fallen branches as she trudged through the forest. She was searching to discover a lost valley. Legend said it was somewhere nearby. She plodded on angrily because she had searched for days, unsuccessfully. She was beginning to think she was on a wild goose chase. It was so hot, sticky and humid that she decided to have a rest. She found a fallen log and sat down heavily. In the silence that followed, she could suddenly hear the unmistakable sound of running water over a waterfall. It was her hidden valley!

**Rule**

An **exclamation** is a word or sentence that shows strong emotion, or gives a warning or command. It ends in an exclamation mark.

*Stop!* *Look at that!* *I love it!*

**1** Read *Search for the Lost Valley*. Underline three **exclamations**.

**2** Write an **exclamation** for Alex to shout as she:

stomped on a fallen branch ______________________________

plodded angrily ______________________________

heard the waterfall ______________________________

**3** Write an **exclamation** for each picture.

______________________________ ______________________________

______________________________ ______________________________



*Grammar Rules! Student Book 3* (ISBN 9780655092438) © Tanya Gibb

Some **adverbs** add meaning to **verbs** by telling how.

*quickly suddenly happily busily carefully*

Adverbs can also tell where. *here there up down*

**4** Write five **adverbs** ending in *–ly* from *Search for the Lost Valley.*

______________________________________________

**5** Use an **adverb** from the box to complete each sentence.

| fiercely<br>wildly<br>down<br>carefully |
|---|

The children sat ______________.

The wind blew ______________.

The child carried the puppy ______________.

The lion growled ______________.

**6** Find and circle the verbs *stomped, trudged* and *plodded* in *Search for the Lost Valley*. What do these **action verbs** tell you about Alex's attitude?

______________________________________________

**7** Write two **adverbials** that tell you where Alex walked in *Search for the Lost Valley*. Hint! Look for prepositional phrases.

______________________________________________

Rule

**Onomatopoeia** is the name for words that imitate sounds.

Onomatopoeia words can help to add atmosphere to a narrative.

*bang crash pop fizz slurp kerplunk*

**8** Find two **onomatopoeia** words in *Search for the Lost Valley.* ______________ ______________

**9** Write an **onomatopoeia** word for a sound made by each thing.

a dog ______________ a cat ______________

a snake ______________ sausages frying in a pan ______________

**Try it yourself!**

Write a **narrative** of your own. Include **onomatopoeia** words to represent sounds. Add **exclamations** to show when characters are angry, excited or surprised. Use **adverbs** to tell how actions happen.

Unit 12

# Revision

**1** Write the **contractions**.

cannot ____________ he is ____________

would not ____________ I am ____________

you will ____________ do not ____________

they are ____________ it will ____________

**2** Circle the correct **verb** for the **subject** of each sentence.

A kookaburra (laugh/laughs).

Kookaburras (laugh/laughs).

Amira (eat/eats) faster than me.

They (read/reads) more often than me.

**3** Write an **adverbial** to complete each sentence.

I like to swim ______________________________.

I wear a hat ______________________________.

The mice jumped ______________________________.

I keep my tools ______________________________.

**4** Write two **adjectives** to describe each **noun**.

______________ ______________ chimpanzee

______________ ______________ banana

______________ ______________ gadget

**5** Choose a **relating verb** from the box to complete each sentence.

| is | was | have | are |
|---|---|---|---|

Elephants ____________ trunks.

Whales ____________ mammals.

Igor ____________ my friend.

I ____________ on the phone.

**6** Cross out the incorrect **personal pronoun** in each sentence.

They will take me with (they/them) to the park.

(She/Her) is a great goalkeeper.

(It/He) is a good cook.

The book is Billy's. Give (it/them) back.

Nonna went skydiving with (him/he).

**7** Write an **exclamation** that shows:

surprise ______________________________

a warning ______________________________


Grammar Rules! Student Book 3 (ISBN 9780655092438) © Tanya Gibb

**8** Add a **possessive apostrophe** to the noun in brackets to complete each sentence.

(Irina) *Irina's* batting is the best.

That's (Ross) ____________ ball.

That's my (teacher) ____________ new desk.

The (team) ____________ win was amazing.

(Xiao) ____________ homework is on his bed.

The (dogs) ____________ barking annoyed us.

**9** Use a **conjunction** from the box to complete each sentence.

| so<br>and<br>or<br>because |
|---|

I won't be able to sleep ____________ I am excited.

It's Dom's birthday ____________ I will make him a cake.

I made chocolate cake ____________ Ariana made Anzac biscuits.

You can have custard ____________ you can have ice cream.

**10** Use a **conjunction** from the box to join each pair of sentences. Write the new sentences.

| because except |
|---|

I love playing netball. I am a good goal shooter.

________________________________________________

It can come inside. The dog cannot come inside when it has muddy feet.

________________________________________________

**11** Write the **plural** of each **singular noun** so that there is more than one.

person ____________ shoe ____________ monkey ____________

**12** Write the **singular** of each **plural noun** so that there is only one of each thing.

teeth ____________ cookies ____________ wishes ____________

**13** Use an **adverb** from the box to complete each sentence.

| happily<br>slowly<br>quickly<br>lazily |
|---|

The old cat yawned ____________.

The children played ____________.

The birthday cake was eaten ____________.

The tortoise plodded ____________ across the sand.

Unit 13

Quoted speech, saying verbs

This text is a **discussion**. Each person makes statements that tell their point of view.

# Trampolines

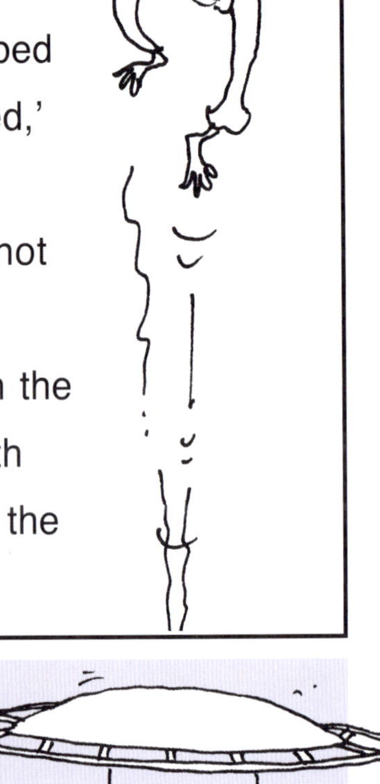

'Dad,' asked Henry, 'do you think the trampoline was a good invention?'

'I'd say that jumping on a trampoline is great exercise, as much fun as jumping on the bed but definitely safer than jumping on the bed,' Dad suggested. 'What do you think?'

'I really like jumping on the bed but I'm not allowed,' reminded Henry.

'You certainly are NOT allowed to jump on the bed. Jumping on the bed is dangerous with all the furniture nearby, so it's just as well the trampoline was invented,' lectured Dad.

**Rule**

**Quoted speech** is the actual speech someone says. It is written inside **quotation (speech) marks.**

*'What do you think?' asked Dad.*

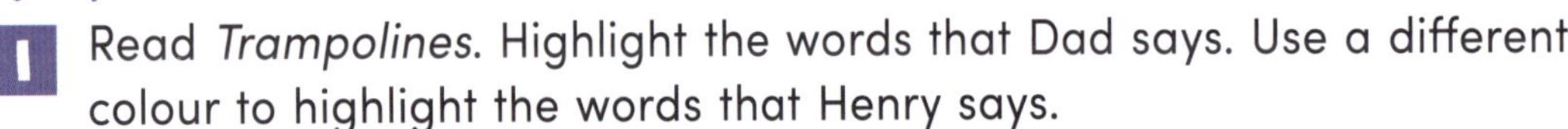

1. Read *Trampolines*. Highlight the words that Dad says. Use a different colour to highlight the words that Henry says.

2. Work with a partner. One of you say Dad's speech. One of you say Henry's speech. Then add some extra **questions** and **statements** to their **discussion**.

3. Write what Henry might say next as **quoted speech**.

________________________________________________

4. Write what Dad might say next as **quoted speech**.

________________________________________________

5. Add **quotation marks** to show which words are said. The quotation marks enclose any other punctuation marks. You can use single or double quotation marks.

I want a turn! shouted Billy.

That's so funny, giggled Marie.

Dad whispered, Santa Claus might bring a trampoline.

Can I have a turn? begged Yan.



*Grammar Rules! Student Book 3* (ISBN 9780655092438) © Tanya Gibb

**6** Write the **saying verbs** used in *Trampolines* for

Dad's speech ____________________ ____________________

Henry's speech ____________________ ____________________

**7** Circle the **saying verbs** in the box.

| whispered | yelled | swam | whined | laughed | asked | peeped |
|---|---|---|---|---|---|---|

Use one of the **saying verbs** in the box in a sentence of your own.

________________________________________________________________

**Tip**

**Adjectives**, **verbs** and **adverbs** show a speaker's or writer's **evaluation** of a topic and can influence the way a listener or reader thinks about a topic.

*hilarious film* *brave explorer* *Rasha sighed wearily.*

**8** What is Dad's opinion about trampolines?

________________________________________________________________

What is Dad's opinion about jumping on the bed?

________________________________________________________________

**9** Find three **contractions** in *Trampolines*.

____________________ ____________________ ____________________

**10** Write **contractions** for the words.

is not ________________ can not ________________

would have ________________ should have ________________

I will ________________ you will ________________

**Try it yourself!**

Discuss your favourite game or activity with a partner. Record part of the **discussion**. Use **quotation marks** to show what was said. Use a variety of **saying verbs**.

Unit 14

Point of view, emotive words, modal verbs and adverbs

This text is from a **narrative**. It includes a conversation where one character is trying to **persuade** the other to do something. Each person's speech is a new paragraph.

# THE THING INSIDE

'No Deni, I really don't want to go in there,' argued Amy.

'Don't be a chicken. We might discover treasure, and it will be fun,' Deni fumed.

'You've heard the stories about that house! What if they're true? Also, it's trespassing,' Amy explained, with her arms folded in front of her.

'What if? What if? What if? Look, the fact is, there is absolutely no such thing as a ghost,' Deni announced convincingly. 'So, stay here or come with me but I'm going in.'

Deni walked up the front steps of the derelict old house. The floorboards creaked and groaned at her every step. She stopped at the front door and turned back towards Amy.

'Well?' she asked, raising her eyebrows.

**Tip** **Body language** and **voice** are often used in arguments to reinforce the point of view. Body language includes gestures and facial expressions. Voice includes volume, pace and tone (the sound of your voice).

**1** Read *The Thing Inside*. Highlight the words that Deni says. Use a different colour to highlight what Amy says.

**2** Work with a partner. One of you say Deni's speech. One of you say Amy's speech. Use **body language** and **voice** to reinforce their points of view.

**3** What **body language** does Amy use in *The Thing Inside*?

______________________________________________________________

What do you think her **body language** means?

______________________________________________________________



*Grammar Rules! Student Book 3* (ISBN 9780655092438) © Tanya Gibb

**4** What **body language** does Deni use in *The Thing Inside*?

______________________________

What do you think her **body language** means?

______________________________

**5** Write Amy's point of view and reasons. Write Deni's point of view and reasons.

| **Amy** | **Deni** |
|---|---|
| ______________ | ______________ |
| ______________ | ______________ |

Would you prefer Amy or Deni as a friend? Why?

______________________________

**Rule**

**Modal verbs** (e.g. *should, might, must, will, can*) and **adverbs** (e.g. *possibly, probably, always, rarely*) are used to make statements more or less forceful, certain or convincing.

*You might.* *You must not.*

*You probably should.* *You definitely shouldn't.*

**6** Tick the sentence in each pair that makes a stronger argument.

| | |
|---|---|
| I really love pizzas. ☐ | I love pizzas. ☐ |
| I want to go. ☐ | I think I want to go. ☐ |
| It's probably haunted. ☐ | It's definitely haunted. ☐ |
| It might not be yours. ☐ | It is not yours. ☐ |

**7** What might the *thing* inside be? What could happen next in the narrative?

______________________________

______________________________

Work with a partner. Choose a topic to **argue** about. Take opposite points of view. Express your points of view very strongly but respectfully. Use **modal verbs** and **adverbs**, **voice** and **body language** to look and sound convincing.

Unit 15

Commas, possessive pronouns, word families

This text is part of a biography. A biography tells about a person's life.

# Jane Goodall

Jane Goodall is famous for her discoveries about wild chimpanzees in Tanzania, Africa.

Jane began studying chimpanzee behaviour in 1960. She was the first person to notice wild chimpanzees make and use tools. She saw the chimps strip leaves off sticks and poke the sticks into termite mounds, digging out the termites to eat. Until Jane's discovery, it was thought that only humans made or used tools. Jane also discovered that chimpanzees feel emotions and have personalities. No scientists had ever noted that before.

Jane later founded charities for wildlife research and to save wild chimpanzees and their habitat.

**1** Read *Jane Goodall*. What did Jane discover about chimpanzees?

________________________________________

________________________________________

**2** Why do you think Jane Goodall set up a charity to save the chimpanzees' habitat?

________________________________________

**Possessive pronouns** are pronouns that show possession.

*mine ours yours theirs his hers its*

*That hat is mine. The forest is theirs. These seats are ours.*

**3** Write a **possessive pronoun** on each line.

Jane's discovery was important. The credit for the discovery is ______________.

Those chimpanzees think that termite mound is ______________.



*Grammar Rules! Student Book 3* (ISBN 9780655092438) © Tanya Gibb

**Commas** separate items in a series. *Bring pens, pencils, paper and a ruler.*
**Commas** separate quoted speech. *'Hello,' said Madison.* OR *Madison said, 'Hello.'*

**4** Rewrite each sentence with correct **punctuation**.

how did jane become interested in chimpanzees

______________________________

chimpazees eat fruit seeds nuts flowers and insects

______________________________

id like to help save bilbies from extinction said lachie

______________________________

elijah swiftly overtook jackson mo and jade in the race

______________________________

**5** In *Jane Goodall*, find the sentence *No scientists had ever noted that before.* What does the word *that* refer to?

______________________________

**6** Write an **adverb** from the box on each line.

| clearly<br>swiftly<br>famously<br>cleverly |
|---|

The chimp ____________ poked the stick in the mound.
The termites ____________ ran out of the mound.
Jane ____________ understood the need for wild animal protection.
Jane ____________ discovered that chimps make and use tools.

Words in a family have the same base. *hope, hopes, hopeful, hopefully, hopeless*

**7** Write a **word family** for *discover*.

______________________________

______________________________

A **biography** is an account of someone's life written by someone else.
An **autobiography** is when someone creates an account of their own life.
Create your autobiography.

This **advertisement** uses **emotive words** to persuade people to buy a product.

# Wiz Bang 3000 Kitchen Hand!

Have you ever needed a spare hand in the kitchen?

Do you often run out of time to chop your food?

Do you ever run out of time to cook your food?

Do you ever run out of time to clean up the mess and do the dishes?

Do you ever wonder if you will have enough time to eat your food?

We now have the answer for you:

**The WIZ BANG 3000 KITCHEN HAND!**

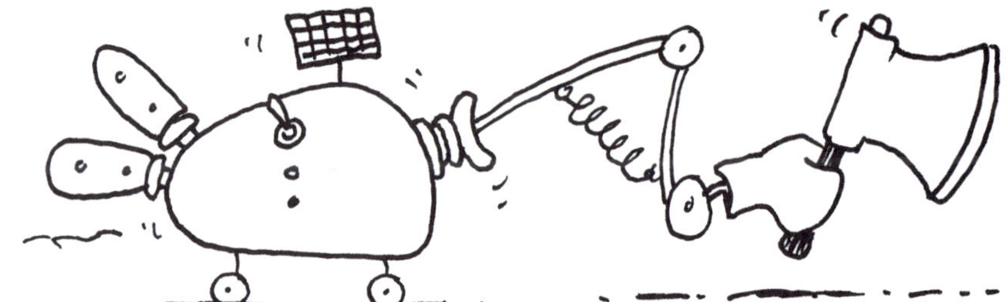

It chops, cooks, cleans and also feeds you your food.

Just ask for a meal from your WIZ BANG 3000 KITCHEN HAND and it will do everything.

**Be quick!** The WIZ BANG 3000 KITCHEN HAND has almost sold out.

**Hurry!** Get this **amazing** invention today!

 **Don't miss out! Buy now!** 

**Tip** **Emotive words** are used in advertisements to persuade people to buy something.

**1** Read *Wiz Bang 3000 Kitchen Hand!*. Underline the **emotive words** that might convince a reader to buy one straight away.

**2** *Wiz Bang 3000 Kitchen Hand!* uses the **emotive words** *'Don't miss out'*. How do you feel when you miss out on something that you really want?

________________________________________

________________________________________

A **command** is a sentence that tells someone to do something.
A command often begins with a verb. *Wash your hands.*

**3** Write five **commands** used in *Wiz Bang 3000 Kitchen Hand!*.

**4** What does the advertisement claim that the Wiz Bang 3000 Kitchen Hand can do?

**5** Tick the statements that show certainty.

- ☐ I will have a lunch order today.
- ☐ You might like to come.
- ☐ You must hug your teddy.
- ☐ I might have toast for breakfast.
- ☐ They will be late.

**6** The first part of the advertisement asks the reader a series of questions. Talk with a partner. What is the purpose of the questions?

**7** In *Wiz Bang 3000 Kitchen Hand!* circle the **personal pronouns** that address the reader.

**8** Find the **personal pronouns** that refer to the Wiz Bang 3000 Kitchen Hand. Underline them in red.

**9** Find the **personal pronoun** that refers to the makers of the Wiz Bang 3000 Kitchen Hand. Underline it in blue.

Remember the rule on page 12.

Write an **advertisement** for a household appliance. Use a real appliance, such as a toaster or an electric toothbrush, or invent a new appliance. Use **modal verbs** and **adverbs** and **emotive words** to convince people to buy your appliance.

# Unit 17

Articles, adjectives that compare

The purpose of this text is to describe bush tucker and persuade the reader to try it.

## BUSH TUCKER

Bush tucker is native Australian food. Bush tucker has been used by First Nations Australians for tens of thousands of years for food and medicines. Bush tucker is sometimes called bush food.

Witchetty grubs are one of the most famous kinds of bush tucker. Witchetty grubs are a very healthy food. They have a nutty taste.

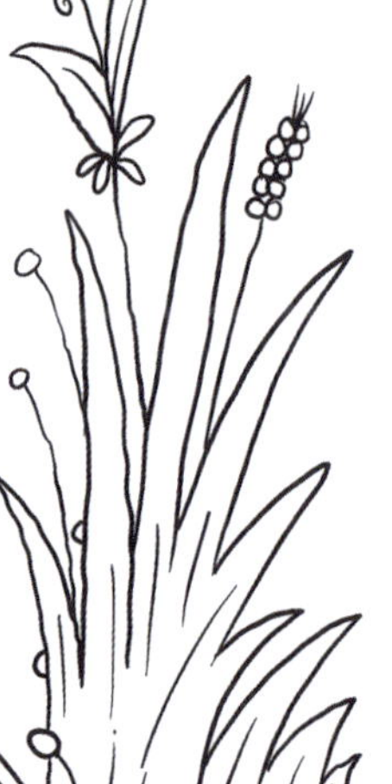

Pepperberry and saltbush (tyulern) are bush foods. They taste just like salt and pepper but are healthier.

A very popular kind of bush tucker is the Davidson's plum or ooray. Ooray are a darker purple than other plums and they make the best jam.

**Tip** Remember the rule about **noun groups** with **articles** on page 15.

**1** Read *Bush Tucker.* Underline four **noun groups** that begin with an **article**.

**2** Circle the correct **article** in each **sentence**.

I tried ( a / an ) Davidson's plum.

It had ( a / an ) amazingly intense flavour.

It had ( a / an ) dark purple colour.

( The / An / A ) plum was cut in half.

( The / A / An ) Davidson's plum jam was delicious.

**3** Which bush tucker does the writer of *Bush Tucker* think tastes like nuts?

_______________________________________________



*Grammar Rules! Student Book 3* (ISBN 9780655092438) © Tanya Gibb

# Grammar Rules!

______________________ 's Writing Log

## 1 Plan

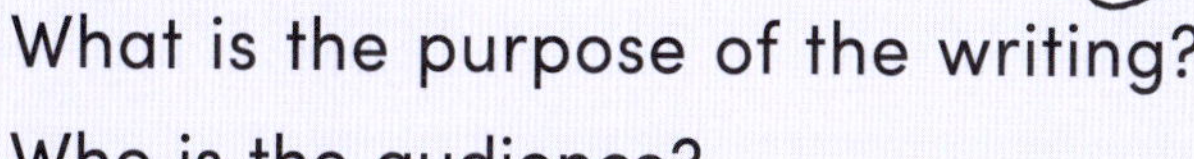

What is the purpose of the writing?
Who is the audience?
What type of text and text form will you use? How can you enhance the presentation?
Gather ideas or research the topic, including using online and digital sources.

## 2 Draft

Gather and organise your ideas.
Use a graphic organiser or digital tools.
Compose your text.

## 3 Edit/Revise

Check your work for meaning, clarity and precision.
Is the structure and sequencing appropriate?
Check layout, paragraphing and sentence structures.
Check topic specific vocabulary.
Ask for help to improve meaning and precision.

## 4 Proofread

Check grammar and punctuation.
Check homonyms are correct.
Use online dictionaries to check spelling.

## 5 Publish

Use layout and visual features.
Use digital tools.
Reflect on your work and your text.

Create symbols for a rating scale. Then each time you finish a piece of writing, record it in the log.

## My rating scale

| Symbol | Meaning |
| --- | --- |
| | Help! |
| | A good start. |
| | I have the basics covered. |
| | I'm beyond the basics. |
| | Brilliant! |

Do you need some ideas for other text forms to try? Look at the back page!

| Date | Write the title of your text. | Text purpose and structure | Audience |
| --- | --- | --- | --- |
| Write the date. | Write the title of your piece. | e.g. recount/ email | Who were you writing <u>for</u> or <u>to</u>? |
| | | | |
| | | | |
| | | | |
| | | | |
| | | | |
| | | | |
| | | | |
| | | | |
| | | | |
| | | | |
| | | | |
| | | | |
| | | | |
| | | | |
| | | | |
| | | | |
| | | | |
| | | | |
| | | | |
| | | | |
| | | | |
| | | | |



*Grammar Rules! Student Book 3* (ISBN 9780655092438) © Tanya Gibb

| Language features | My rating | Where to next? |
|---|---|---|
| ist the main grammar and other language eatures that you used. | Record your rating. | What will you try next?<br>How could you improve your writing?<br>Does your teacher have any comments? |
| | | |
| | | |
| | | |
| | | |
| | | |
| | | |
| | | |
| | | |
| | | |
| | | |
| | | |
| | | |
| | | |
| | | |
| | | |
| | | |
| | | |
| | | |
| | | |
| | | |
| | | |
| | | |
| | | |

# I've tried these types of texts and text forms . . .

## Narrative

- [ ] Poem
- [ ] Retelling a story
- [ ] Other ______________

## Recount

- [ ] Letter/email
- [ ] News article
- [ ] A real or imagined event
- [ ] Other ______________

## Description

- [ ] Poem
- [ ] Wanted poster/lost poster
- [ ] Letter
- [ ] Advertisement
- [ ] Narrative/story

## Response

- [ ] Diary
- [ ] Review (book, concert, excursion)
- [ ] Poem
- [ ] Other ______________

## Persuasion

- [ ] Debate
- [ ] Argument/speech
- [ ] Advertisement
- [ ] Poster
- [ ] Poem
- [ ] Other ______________

## Informative

- [ ] Information report
- [ ] Brochure/poster
- [ ] Autobiography
- [ ] Other ______________

## Explanation

- [ ] Cycle diagram/flow chart
- [ ] Poster

## Procedure

- [ ] Recipe
- [ ] Instructions
- [ ] Rules
- [ ] Directions

## Discussion

- [ ] Conversation
- [ ] Narrative dialogue
- [ ] Formal interview
- [ ] Other ______________


*Grammar Rules! Student Book 3* (ISBN 9780655092438) © Tanya Gibb

**Adjectives** change form when used to compare things.
When comparing two things we often add *–er*.

*long→longer*

When comparing more than two things we often add *–est*.

*long→longer→longest*

**4** Write the different forms for each **adjective** to compare things.

| long | longer | longest |
|---|---|---|
| tall | | |
| sweet | | |
| small | | |
| good | | |

Some **longer adjectives** need a different way to show **comparison**.
Adjectives with more than two syllables usually use:

- *more* for two things *The rose is more beautiful than the dandelion.*
- *most* for more than two things *The rose is the most beautiful flower in the garden.*

**5** Complete each **sentence** with *more* or *most.*

Wattle seeds are ____________ delicious than linseeds.

Wattle seeds are the ____________ delicious seeds to use in cakes.

Witchetty grubs are the ____________ famous bush tucker.

Witchetty grubs are ____________ famous than pepperberries.

**6** Write the **comparing** forms of these **adjectives**. Hint! You'll find them in *Bush Tucker.*

dark ____________________ healthy ____________________

Write a **description** of an animal or food. Use **noun groups** with **articles** and **adjectives** to build up your description. Be careful to use the right form when using adjectives to compare.

# Unit 18 Revision

**1** Add **quotation (speech) marks** around the **quoted speech**.

Take me with you! screamed Louie.

I would like to go, too, suggested Rhami.

I think that's a good idea, replied Pop.

Marty sniggered, Good.

**2** What does Dad say? Use **quotation marks**.

______________________________

______________________________

What does Mum say? Use **quotation marks**.

______________________________

______________________________

**3** Write a **contraction** for each word or word group. Hint! Remember to use an **apostrophe**.

I am ____________

I have ____________

do not ____________

cannot ____________

could have ____________

is not ____________

**4** Which sentences express the greatest **certainty**? Tick one box in each row.

I am very pleased. ☐ I am pleased. ☐

I might go. ☐ I will go. ☐

I think I lost my ball. ☐ I lost my ball. ☐

Dad might be home soon. ☐ Dad will be home soon. ☐

**5** Tick the **commands**.

Order your lunch by 9 am. ☐

Don't walk on the grass. ☐

Have you thrown out your rubbish? ☐

Put on your sunhat. ☐

**6** Circle the **modal verb** in each sentence.

You must sit.

We might go for a walk.

You could try this plum.

We should go for a walk.



*Grammar Rules! Student Book 3* (ISBN 9780655092438) © Tanya Gibb

**7** Add a **possessive apostrophe** to the noun in brackets for each sentence to show possession.

(Lee) ____________ painting

(Nina) ____________ desk

(Dad) ____________ sock

the (team) ____________ win

(Hilda) ____________ brother

(parents) ____________ applause

**8**

Try Jitto. You might like it.

Buy Jetto. It tastes great and is good for you.

Which poster above is more **persuasive**? Give reasons for your choice.

_______________________________________________

_______________________________________________

**9** Complete the table with **adjectives** that compare.

| tall | taller | tallest |
|---|---|---|
| loud | | |
| smart | | |
| kind | | |

**10** Write the correct form of the **adjective** in brackets.

One clown was ________________ (funny) than the other.

The clown in the red hat was the ________________ (funny).

My laboratory was ________________ (tidy) than my assistant's.

My laboratory is the ________________ (tidy) laboratory in the building.

**11** Write a strong **argument** for Anton to respond to Lena.
'Anton, you have to do my homework. I don't have time,' said Lena.

_______________________________________________

_______________________________________________

# Haiku

Haiku poems were invented in Japan.
A haiku poem has 17 syllables in three lines.

Line 1 has 5 syllables.
Line 2 has 7 syllables.
Line 3 has 5 syllables.

Traditional haiku poems are usually about nature. Modern haiku poems can be about any topic and poets can vary the number of syllables they use.

**1** Snow floats softly down
whispering on my cold skin.
Winter is here now.

**2** See the spring garden.
Listen to magpies warbling.
Flowers fill the air.

**3** Raining cats and dogs.
Puddles grow on swampy lawn.
I watch from inside.

**4** As fast as lightning,
the eagle swoops on its prey.
Today it will eat.

This text is **informative**. It describes the form of a haiku poem and includes examples of the poem.

**Rule**

**Imagery** means using words that appeal to the senses and help a reader or listener create a picture in their mind.

**1** What picture do you see in your mind when reading poem 1?

_______________________________________________

**2** Write three words from poem 1 that tell you about the weather.

______________ ______________ ______________

**3** What human behaviour does the poet say snow can do in poem 1? ______________

**4** Which two words tell you snow is quiet in poem 1? ______________ ______________

**5** Which senses does poem 2 appeal to?

______________ ______________ ______________



*Grammar Rules! Student Book 3* (ISBN 9780655092438) © Tanya Gibb

An **idiom** is an expression that means something different from the meaning of the words.
*ankle biter* *spit the dummy* *put a sock in it*

**6** Write the **idiom** used in poem 3. What does it mean?

______________________________

**7** Draw a line to link each **idiom** with its meaning.

| | |
|---|---|
| fit as a fiddle | something worthwhile |
| shake a leg | die |
| nothing to sneeze at | very healthy |
| a dog's breakfast | stranded |
| kick the bucket | hurry up |
| high and dry | a mess |

**8** What do you think the *swampy lawn* in poem 3 feels like and sounds like? Use **adjectives** of your own.

______________________________
______________________________
______________________________
______________________________
______________________________

**9** What does the poet reveal in the last line of poem 3?

______________________________

**Tip**

A **simile** is a figure of speech. Something is spoken of as being like something else. The words *like* or *as* are used.
*as quick as a fox* *snarled like a tiger*

**10** Write the simile in poem 4. ______________________________

**11** Draw a line to complete each **simile**.

| | |
|---|---|
| slept like | a feather |
| as light as | a log |
| the ship tossed like | a bee |
| as busy as | a cork |

**12** Find five **adverbs** or **adverbials** that tell where or when in the haiku poems.

______________________________
______________________________
______________________________

Interview teachers and family members. Ask them to suggest **idioms** and **similes**. Write a poem that uses one or more of their suggestions. Or, create a poster or multimodal text that illustrates one or more.

Unit 20 Connectives, facts and opinions

This is a **speech**. The speaker's purpose is to **persuade** people to do something.

# Recycle!

Good morning. I'm here today to tell you how important it is to recycle mobile phones.

Firstly, recycling a mobile phone means that all the materials that have gone into making the phone can be recovered and used again instead of wasted. This protects nature because we won't have to mine for new resources.

Secondly, recycling helps save wildlife. For example, coltan is a mineral used in smartphones. Mining for coltan in the Congo Basin in Africa is destroying gorilla habitat. Some gorilla species are in danger of extinction because of loss of habitat.

Additionally, when mobile phones end up in landfill, their batteries leak harmful toxins into the environment.

Help the planet! Recycle your old mobile phone.

**Rule**

**Connectives** are words and phrases that help to sequence ideas across a text. They can be **adverbs**, **conjunctions** or **phrases**.

*firstly* *finally* *as well as* *alternatively* *although* *when* *while*

**1** Read *Recycle!*. Circle the **connectives**. Hint! These give the text a logical sequence.

**2** How many reasons does the speaker give to support recycling mobile phones? ☐

**3** Number the sentences from 1 to 5 to show the sequence. Hint! The **connectives** will help you.

☐ So, choose sandwiches for lunch today.

☐ To begin with, sandwiches are healthy.

☐ Finally, sandwiches can easily be packed for school lunches.

☐ Sandwiches are good for lunch.

☐ In addition, sandwiches are economical.

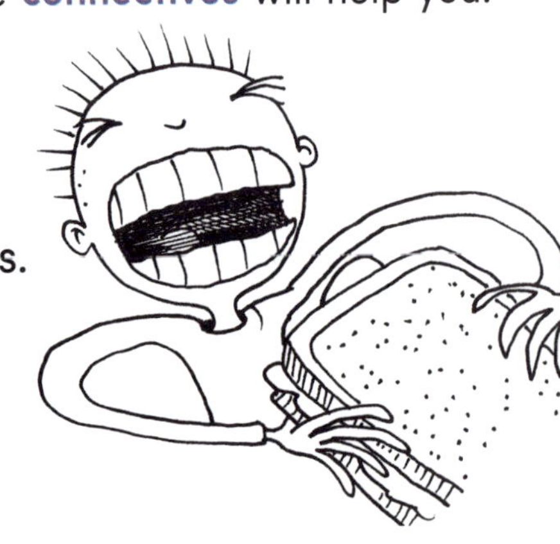



*Grammar Rules! Student Book 3* (ISBN 9780655092438) © Tanya Gibb

**4** Use the **connectives** from the box to complete the text below. Use a capital letter if it begins a sentence.

| in addition | finally | while | secondly | firstly |
|---|---|---|---|---|

I believe that television is unhealthy.

_______________, it encourages people to sit around and not exercise.

_______________, people tend to eat more _______________ they watch television.

_______________, the shows on television do not stimulate the brain.

_______________, television stops families from having conversations.

People should watch less television.

**Statements** can express **facts** or **opinions**. Opinions can include words that are emotive.

Fact: *Anzac biscuits are made with oats.*

Opinion: *Anzac biscuits are best when they are soft and gooey.*

**5** Link each statement to FACT or OPINION.

There's a wattle tree in Aunty's yard.

Wattle trees have beautiful yellow flowers.

Pop's poodle is cute.

The whale stranding was a tragedy.

Dolphins love to help people.

FACT

OPINION

Pete's mobile phone is broken.

Whales are mammals.

Dolphins are smarter than orcas.

**6** *Recycle!* ends with a call to action. Write it here.

_______________________________________________

Write a **speech** to **persuade** class members to do something. It could be about reducing litter, raising money for a charity, donating old toys, joining a team or anything else. Use words that are **emotive**. Use **connectives** to link your ideas logically. End with a call to action. Ask a peer to help edit your work. Rehearse your speech before presenting it to the class.

Unit 21

Quoted speech, stereotypes

# PROFESSOR SNODGRASS FAILS AGAIN

This imaginative text is a comic strip **narrative**. It uses speech balloons to show what the character is saying.

**Tip**

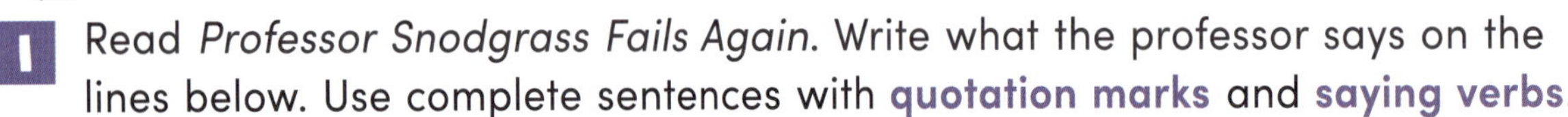

In comic strips, **quoted speech** is shown in speech balloons. Quotation marks are not needed.

**1** Read *Professor Snodgrass Fails Again.* Write what the professor says on the lines below. Use complete sentences with **quotation marks** and **saying verbs**.

______________________________________________

______________________________________________

______________________________________________

**2** What would you say to Professor Snodgrass if you met him? Write your speech using **quotation marks**.

______________________________________________

______________________________________________



*Grammar Rules! Student Book 3* (ISBN 9780655092438) © Tanya Gibb

**3** Write speech inside each speech balloon.

**4** Read out loud the made-up term *'curus maximus stinkolata footitis'*. Have a guess what each word could mean.

---

Cartoons and comic strips often use **stereotypes**. A stereotype is a caricature or an oversimplification. The image of Professor Snodgrass is a stereotype, not a true-to-life image of a professor.

**5** Draw a line to connect each description to either a real-life scientist or a stereotype.

| | | | |
|---|---|---|---|
| works in a laboratory or in the field | male only | | may or may not wear glasses or contact lenses |
| | any gender | | |
| works in a laboratory only | **real-life scientist** | **stereotype scientist** | wears crooked, broken glasses |
| has no friends | nutty and mad | works safely | does crazy experiments and always causes explosions |
| works alone | intelligent | | |

Create a comic strip of your own to tell a narrative. Base your comic strip on a character that you can **stereotype** (e.g. brave hero, nosy neighbour, villain). Use speech balloons for what the characters say.

# Unit 22 Emotive words, synonyms, abstract nouns

This article **reports** events that have happened. It uses **emotive words** to make the events seem more interesting.

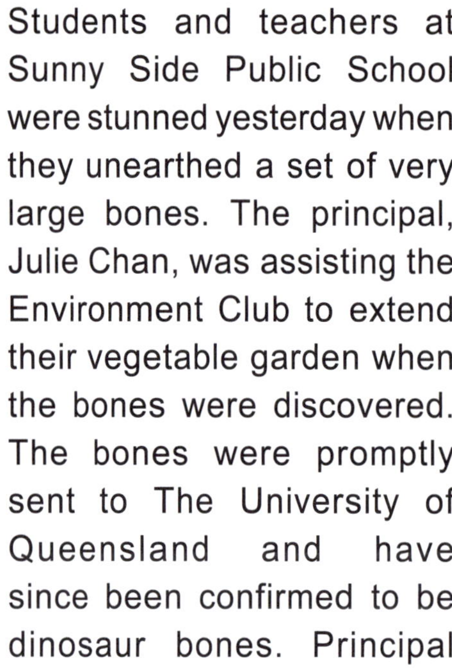

Daily News 7 August

## DINOSAUR FOUND AT LOCAL SCHOOL

Students and teachers at Sunny Side Public School were stunned yesterday when they unearthed a set of very large bones. The principal, Julie Chan, was assisting the Environment Club to extend their vegetable garden when the bones were discovered. The bones were promptly sent to The University of Queensland and have since been confirmed to be dinosaur bones. Principal Chan said that the school community is very excited to have uncovered these incredible pieces of history.

**Tip** News items sometimes use **emotive words** to sensationalise the writing. This creates interest.

**1** Read *Dinosaur Found at Local School*. If you just read the headline, what would you think happened at the school?

**2** What would be a more accurate but less sensational headline?

**3** Which headline do you prefer and why?

**CHILDREN DIG UP DINOSAUR**

**DINOSAUR IN VEGIE PATCH**

**DINOSAUR FOUND AT LOCAL SCHOOL**

**DINOSAUR DISCOVERY**

*Grammar Rules! Student Book 3* (ISBN 9780655092438) © Tanya Gibb

**Synonyms** are words that have similar meanings.
*beautiful/pretty*  *small/tiny*  *coarse/rough*  *clever/smart*

**4** Find **synonyms** in the news report for the following words.

shocked ______________ immediately ______________ uncovered ______________

helping ______________ found ______________ thrilled ______________

huge ______________ amazing ______________ expand ______________

**5** Find the word in the news report that means 'dug up'. ______________

**6** What are the *incredible pieces of history* in the news report?

______________________________________________

**7** Find and write four **adjectives** used in the news report.

______________________________________________

**8** Find the **adverb** that ends in *-ly* in the news report. ______________

**9** Circle the **modal verbs** in each sentence.

'There might be more bones,' suggested Ulrike.

'There must be!' declared Jon.

'We could dig for some,' offered Evan.

'We should come back after school,' said Izzy.

Which child above makes the strongest statement? ______________

Nouns can be **abstract**. *peace hatred*
Add a **suffix** to an **adjective** to create an abstract noun. *sleepy sleepiness*

**10** Find and circle the **abstract noun** *history* in *Dinosaur Found at Local School.*

Write a news article that reports about something that has happened at your school. Use **emotive language** to make the events sound exciting. Don't forget to write an attention-grabbing headline.

# The Discovery

This text is the beginning of a story. It introduces the **main character** and sets the scene for events in the plot.

Ella's family was camping in the mountains. One night, after taking her little sister to their parents' tent, Ella noticed something colourful stuck in the tree branches above the camp site. It was too dark to see properly, so she decided to wait until morning to have a better look. The next morning, as soon as she woke, Ella climbed the tree to see what was hidden in the branches. It was a high climb, but eventually she reached the section of the tree that held the object. She discovered that it was a very small jacket, only big enough for a very tiny person, and there was something in the pocket.

**Rule**

**Verbs** can show when an action happened. This is called **tense**.

| | | |
|---|---|---|
| **past tense** | *She went* | *She has gone.* |
| **present tense** | *She goes.* | *She is going.* |
| **future tense** | *She will go.* | *She might go.* |

**1** Read *The Discovery*. Underline three **adverbials** that tell where. Hint! Look for prepositional phrases.

**2** **Past tense verbs** often end in *–ed*. Circle five past tense verbs in *The Discovery* that end in *–ed*.

**3** Tick a column to show the **tense** of each sentence.

| | Past | Present | Future |
|---|---|---|---|
| I am hungry. | | | |
| I chased the cat. | | | |
| I will go to the park. | | | |
| You are standing in the way. | | | |
| You stepped on my toes. | | | |

*Grammar Rules! Student Book 3* (ISBN 9780655092438) 

The **narrator** of a story can be the author using pronouns *they, he, she* or *them* to tell about the characters (**third-person narrator**). Or, a story can be narrated by one of the characters in the story using pronouns *I, we* or *me* (**first-person narrator**).

**4** *The Discovery* has a **third-person narrator**. Imagine you are Ella, writing the story yourself, as a **first-person narrator**. What are you thinking as you climb the tree and discover the jacket?

________________________________________

________________________________________

________________________________________

**5** Add some other **past tense verbs** to replace *got* in this paragraph.

Ella (got) _______________ down from the tree and (got) _______________ into her tent. She (got) _______________ her sister to hold the jacket while she (got) _______________ her reading glasses from her backpack for a closer look.

**6** What have your learned about Ella's character in the story so far? Circle the **adjectives** you judge to be true about her.

**Ella seems:**

observant timid strong cheeky interested sensible reckless

brave adventurous curious stubborn kind argumentative

Share your selections with a partner. Justify your choices.

**7** Would you like Ella as a friend? Why or why not?

________________________________________

________________________________________

Write a **narrative** of your own. Use words and phrases that show the sequence of events. Use **adjectives** to describe the characters. Ask a classmate to proofread and help edit your work.

# Unit 24 Revision

**1** Use an apostrophe to show **possession**.

The dog belongs to Jude. It is Jude's dog.

The keys belong to Aunty. They are ______________________.

The paw belongs to the cat. It is the ______________________.

The children own the skateboards. They are the ______________________.

The teachers own the cars. They are the ______________________.

**2** Number the sentences from 1 to 5 to show the sequence.

- [ ] Therefore, I recommend soccer to everyone.
- [ ] Firstly, it gives you a lot of exercise.
- [ ] My third point is that it teaches you how to be part of a team.
- [ ] I think soccer is a great sport.
- [ ] Secondly, it teaches you lots of skills.

**3** Write two **facts** and two **opinions** about your class.

| Fact | Opinion |
| --- | --- |
| ______________________ | ______________________ |
| ______________________ | ______________________ |
| ______________________ | ______________________ |

**4** Add **quotation marks** to show **quoted speech**.

Your dad was as fast as lightning when he was your age, said Nonna.

Dad said, Not anymore.

Why not? I asked.

My knee is kaput, replied Dad, sadly.

What's kaput? I asked and Nonna raised her eyebrows.

Guess! said Dad.

*Grammar Rules! Student Book 3* (ISBN 9780655092438) © Tanya Gibb

**5** Imagine that your school principal won the lottery and decided to take the whole school on a holiday to Fiji. Write a news headline about it. Use **emotive words**.

________________________________________________

**6** Find **synonyms** in this text for the words below.

> It's exciting to watch Madison de Rozario compete in wheelchair racing. She is an amazing athlete. Racing wheelchairs have two large wheels at the back and one smaller wheel at the front. Racers need powerful upper bodies to reach speeds of more than 30kmph. It can be dangerous.

strong ____________ competitors ____________ risky ____________

thrilling ____________ incredible ____________ big ____________

**7** Tick a column to show the **tense** of each sentence.

| | Past | Present | Future |
|---|---|---|---|
| I am tired. | | | |
| I fed the hippos. | | | |
| Will we go to the park? | | | |
| You are blocking the doorway. | | | |
| You squashed the banana. | | | |
| We might go to the movies on Saturday. | | | |

**8** Cross out the incorrect **verb**.

I (go/went) to the shop yesterday.

I (bought/will buy) a milkshake later.

Mary (played/plays) cricket last Saturday.

Rami (rid/rode) his bike to school this morning.

**9** Number these sentences from 1 to 4 in time order.

☐ After school, we had gymnastics.

☐ Before lunch, we marked our homework.

☐ After lunch, we had art.

☐ Before school, I went to the library.

# THE BEST NEW INVENTION

A number of amazing inventions have been entered in the Best New Invention Competition.

Many people think the Heli Cooler Hat should win because it keeps people cool on a hot day. The 40-centimetre blades are attached to the top of a sunhat. When the 'on' switch is pressed, the blades whirl around like a fan.

Other people prefer the Santa Claus Detector because it sets off a silent alarm the second Santa Claus falls down the chimney.

Every young child will want a Santa Claus Detector, for sure. However, my vote goes to the Heli Cooler Hat because I think it will be useful every day and it is also great for keeping people sun safe.

This **persuasive** text summarises different points of view. It uses the **conjunction** *because* to link opinions with reasons.

**1** Read *The Best New Invention*. Underline the **noun group** at the beginning of each paragraph.

**Tip** Remember the rule on page 15.

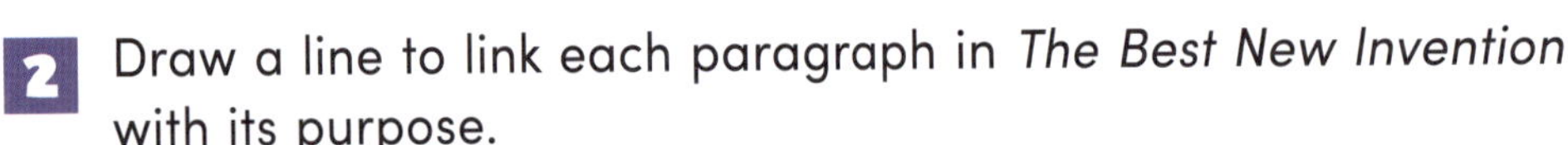

**2** Draw a line to link each paragraph in *The Best New Invention* with its purpose.

| | |
|---|---|
| Paragraph 1 | to present an opinion and give reasons |
| Paragraph 2 | to make a final recommendation or judgement |
| Paragraph 3 | to present a different opinion and give reasons |
| Paragraph 4 | to introduce the topic |

**Rule** **Conjunctions** and other connecting words can link an opinion with a reason or condition and create **complex sentences**.

*because although so however since unless in case otherwise*

**3** Circle the **conjunction** in *The Best New Invention* that links each opinion with a reason.


*Grammar Rules! Student Book 3* (ISBN 9780655092438) © Tanya Gibb

**4** Choose a **conjunction** from the box to join the clauses correctly.

| although | because | otherwise | so | unless |
|---|---|---|---|---|

I like apples better than oranges ________________ they are sweeter.

I'll have the orange ________________ I prefer apples.

You don't like apples ________________ take an orange in your lunch box.

I don't like apples ________________ they are very crisp.

You should eat them before they go bad ________________ they'll be wasted.

**Tip**

Different **modal verbs** and **adverbs** are used for different **audiences** and **purposes**. In an advertisement, it is important to express certainty.

*This is definitely the very best product on the market. You must buy it!*

When interacting with others, it is important to respond respectfully.

*You made some good points but perhaps we could try something else.*

**5** Draw a line to link each comment to the person most likely to say it.

I see what you mean but I'm not sure I agree.

You are absolutely wrong.

I understand what you're saying.

That's a good point but I can't agree.

Maybe you have a point.

That is a stupid suggestion.

Your opinion is ridiculous.

You can't be serious.

I'm not sure I can agree with what you've said.

We should probably think about these ideas a little more.

Thank you for your ideas but I disagree.

disrespectful

respectful

Discuss your favourite gadget or invention with a partner. Listen and comment respectfully. Use words such as *I think, possibly, perhaps*. Record the opinions presented and the reasons for them in a written **discussion**. Use the same structure as in *The Best New Invention*.

This report is **informative**. It provides factual information about the topic. It uses topic-specific terminology.

# Creation Stories

Creation stories are stories that have been told from one First Nations generation to the next for thousands of years. Creation stories teach important lessons about sharing resources, caring for Country and valuing the knowledge of Elders.

The story of a water-holding frog, who greedily drinks all the water in the land, is a creation story of the Gunaikurnai people, as well as other Australian First Nations groups. In some of the stories about the water-guzzling frog, when the frog laughs, the land floods and many creatures drown.

The story of Tiddalick, the greedy frog, is based on a First Nations story.

**1** Read *Creation Stories*. Complete the sentence.

Some creation stories do not have a happy ending because ______________________

______________________________________________

**2** In *Creation Stories*, find and underline four **noun groups** that refer to the frog.

**3** Write the **adverb** in *Creation Stories* that tells how the frog drank. ______________________

**4** Add a **conjunction** to connect the clauses.

First Nations stories are important ______________ they explain people's connection to Country, plants and animals.

**5** Rewrite the sentences with correct punctuation.

the giant frog is molok in some parts of australia said harriet

______________________________________________

different first nations peoples have different creation stories said kaya

______________________________________________



Grammar Rules! Student Book 3 (ISBN 9780655092438) © Tanya Gibb

**Prefixes** are letters or word parts added to the front of words. **Suffixes** are added to the ends of words. They form plurals and show tense. Prefixes and suffixes change word meanings.

*happy–unhappy* *understood–misunderstood* *care–careful–careless*

**6** Add a **prefix** from the box to each word. You can use any prefix twice.

| un | im | il | re | in | non | ir |
|---|---|---|---|---|---|---|

do ______________ send ______________

correct ______________ sense ______________

logical ______________ like ______________

important ______________

**7** Draw a line to match each describing **adjective** with a **noun**.

| | |
|---|---|
| endangered | melody |
| prickly | aunt |
| colourful | forest |
| dense | lorikeet |
| tuneful | cactus |
| thoughtful | numbat |

Rule

A **noun group** can include **adjectives** that show possession, describe and tell number, order or quantity.

*his last apple* *a few goannas* *their first home* *one wise old owl*

**8** Underline all the **adjectives** in the sentences.

'I know a few words in the Gubbi Gubbi language,' declared Rami.

'I know twenty Gubbi Gubbi words,' said Lane, 'including "Wunya Ngulumi!"'

'I speak some Gubbi Gubbi. My knowledge is better than yours,' said Indya.

**9** Complete the paragraph using **adjectives** from the box.

| black | bottom | red | top | yellow | two |
|---|---|---|---|---|---|

The Australian Aboriginal Flag is a rectangle divided into ______________ halves. The ______________ half is ______________ for the people. The ______________ half is ______________ for the earth. The flag has a ______________ sun in the centre.

Try it yourself!

Find a First Nations creation story that you like. Work in a group. Plan how to **retell** or act out the story for the rest of the class. Present the story. Summarise the lesson or moral at the end of your presentation.

This is a **recipe**. Its title tells the goal. It includes a list of ingredients. The method lists steps to follow in sequence.

# Wart, Fester and Carbuncle Remover

## Ingredients

- 1 cup milk
- 100 g grated candle wax
- 1 tablespoon very hot chilli powder
- 10 ml nail polish remover
- 2 cups vinegar

## Method

1. Mix all ingredients into a paste.
2. Apply a thin film of paste over affected areas.
3. Bandage affected areas.
4. Avoid water for four weeks. (This means no baths or showers.)



**1** Read *Wart, Fester and Carbuncle Remover*. Circle the **adjectives** that tell the amount of each ingredient to use.

**2** What do *g* and *ml* mean in the recipe? ______________ ______________

**3** Complete each sentence with a word from the box. Make sure each sentence makes sense.

| enough<br>a pinch<br>200 g<br>1 litre |
|---|

Add ______________ of salt.

Add ______________ water to make a smooth paste.

Add ______________ of sugar.

Stir in ______________ of milk.

**4** Use a dictionary. Write the definition of *carbuncle*.

______________________________________________

Write the definition of *fester* as it is used in the text.

______________________________________________

What is a wart?

______________________________________________

**5** Underline the **number adjectives**.

The third runner is my friend.

A few friends are coming.

I won second prize for my invention.

I have three cats.

Many schools organise excursions to the museum.

A hundred people went to the concert.

**Tip**

The method of a recipe is a series of **commands**. Most commands start with an **action verb**.
Sometimes commands start with an **adverb** that tells how to do something.

**6** Write the **action verbs** in *Wart, Fester and Carbuncle Remover*.

____________ ____________ ____________ ____________

**7** Use an **adverb** from the box to start each **command**.

| carefully | briskly | gently | totally |
|---|---|---|---|

1. ____________ mix all ingredients into a paste.
2. ____________ apply a thin film of paste over affected areas.
3. ____________ bandage affected areas.
4. ____________ avoid water for four weeks.

**8** Would you use the recipe *Warts, Festers and Carbuncle Remover* if you had a wart? Explain.

____________________________________

____________________________________

____________________________________

Create a **recipe** to cure a real sickness or a made-up sickness, such as school fever or breatho stinko o'lot'o. Use **number adjectives** for the amounts of each ingredient. Use an **action verb** or **adverb** at the beginning of each **command**.

This is an **explanation**. An explanation tells how or why something happens. Information is sequenced in time or through cause and effect.

# How the Alarm Bed Works

1. An alarm clock, attached to the head of the bed, rings when it is time for the sleeper to get up.
2. When it rings, the sleeper has five minutes to get out of bed because that alarm starts a five-minute timer in the mattress springs.
3. If the pressure on the mattress springs has not changed when the five minutes are up (in other words, if the sleeper is still in the bed), then a latch at the head of the bed is released. This causes the mattress and bed base to catapult upward.
4. Then the sleeper is ejected from the bed.

**1** What changes the pressure on the mattress springs?

________________________________________

Circle the correct movement of the bed.

When the bed base catapults upward it a) glides on springs b) moves suddenly and quickly or c) rises off the floor.

**Conjunctions** and **adverbs** connect ideas in time or through cause and effect.

*then* *next* *when* *until* *therefore* *however* *if*

**2** Find and circle the words that sequence events in *How the Alarm Bed Works.*

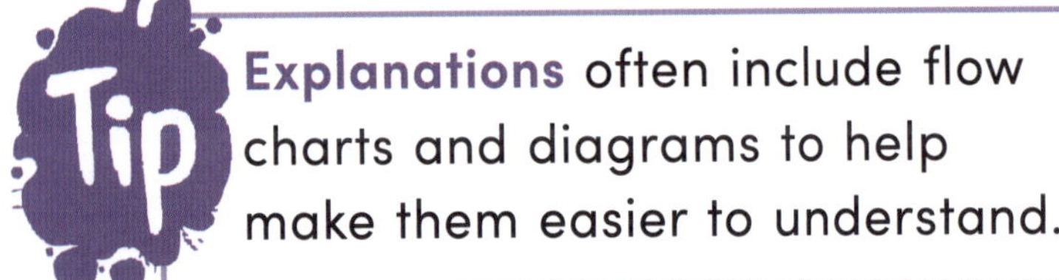


**Explanations** often include flow charts and diagrams to help make them easier to understand.

**3** On spare paper, draw an illustration to match one of the steps in *How the Alarm Bed Works*. Share and discuss your illustration with a partner.

**4** Write a list of things you would need to construct the alarm bed. These things will be **nouns**.

________________________________________

________________________________________

________________________________________

**5** Choose a **conjunction** from the box to join the clauses.

| because<br>then<br>so<br>Unless<br>until |
|---|

Sleep soundly __________ the alarm goes off.

BOING

The alarm bed is effective __________ it gets you out of bed.

__________ you get up within five minutes, the bed will eject you.

Don't go back to sleep __________ the bed base will catapult upward.

Being ejected from bed is not fun __________ don't try to sleep in.

**6** Write the **action verb** for each step in the process.

a. The alarm clock __________.

b. The alarm clock __________ a timer.

c. The latch __________.

d. The mattress and bed base __________.

e. The sleeper is __________.

**Rule**

A **verb group** is a group of words that includes a verb. A verb group might include a **helping verb** (e.g. *is, was, had*), a **modal verb** (e.g. *can, might, should*) or an **adverb** (e.g. *quickly*).

*had been baking* *is going* *has eaten* *will follow* *mustn't go* *gently touched*

**7** Circle the **verb** or **verb group** in each clause.

Anders had been sleeping when the bed ejected him.

Leo was catapulted from his bed this morning.

Evey didn't stay in bed when her alarm started ringing.

Remy might set his alarm bed for 7 o'clock tomorrow.

**8** Use **evaluative words** to write your opinion of the alarm bed and your reasons. Is it useful? Will it work? Will people buy it and use it?

______________________________________________________________

______________________________________________________________

Create an invention of your own. Then write an explanation to tell how it works. Use **connectives** to show time and to show cause and effect. Or, imagine your new alarm bed ejected you early one very cold winter morning. Write your response.

This **informative** text tells the purpose of a device and how to use it. The instructions use **commands** and **action verbs**.

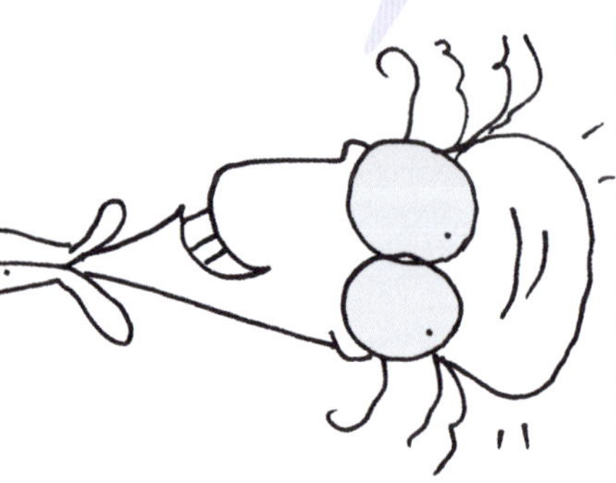

## How to Use the Drolley (or Dog Trolley)

The Drolley (Dog Trolley) allows you to walk a number of dogs at the same time.

1. Attach each dog's lead to a special hook on the Drolley and then push the Drolley to walk the dogs. A brake in the hook activates automatically if any dog pulls too hard.
2. Use the Drolley's plastic suction hose to suck up dog droppings, so they can be treated with environmentally-safe chemicals and then used to fertilise your garden.
3. Store drinking bowls and dog treats in the Drolley's tray, which is located along the side of the Drolley.

**1** Read *How to Use the Drolley (or Dog Trolley)*. Underline four **clauses** that are **commands**. Hint! Remember that every clause has a **verb** or **verb group**.

Sometimes nouns are used as **adjectives** to classify in a noun group.

*timber floor* *basketball match* *ballet shoes* *coconut biscuits*

**2** Underline the **noun groups**. Circle the **adjectives** that classify.

Use the treated dog droppings as fertiliser.

Dog treats can be stored in the tray.

It has a plastic suction hose.

That dog has a leather collar.

It makes an unusual garden fertiliser.

Elkie wore a straw sunhat on her walk.

The rubber wheels made it easy to steer.

*Grammar Rules! Student Book 3* (ISBN 9780655092438) © Tanya Gibb

**3** Choose a **noun** from the box to classify each noun below.

| rain | oak | fruit | tin | chocolate | refrigerator |
|---|---|---|---|---|---|
| hand | marsupial | money | football | | |

________ tree ________ shed ________ truck

________ cloud ________ box ________ cake

________ boot ________ juice ________ bag

________ mouse

**4** Add a **noun group** to each line to complete the sentence.
For example: *A person who teaches is a teacher.*

A person who invents is ________.

A person who performs magic tricks is ________.

A person who studies is ________.

A person who plays a musical instrument is ________.

A person who acts is ________.

A person who conducts an orchestra is ________.

A person who plays the piano is ________.

A person who works in the field of science is ________.

**5** Add a **clause** to complete each sentence.

The Drolley works best when ________

The Drolley topples over if ________

The Drolley's wheels freeze up when ________

The treated dog business is released when ________

Write a **procedure** (instructions) for using a piece of equipment. Or, invent something, describe its features and write instructions for how to use it.

# Unit 30 Revision

**1** Complete each sentence with a **connective/conjunction** from the box. Use a capital letter if the connective begins a sentence.

| so | since | unless | in case | otherwise |
|---|---|---|---|---|

__________ we can't have cake, let's have ice cream.

Take your raincoat __________ it starts to rain.

Start your homework straight away. __________ you won't finish before dinner.

__________ you start now you won't be finished before dinner.

Get your homework finished __________ you can watch some television.

**2** Circle the **connective** in each sentence and then underline the **clauses**.

Harlow is feeling healthier because she is eating more vegetables.

Noah offered to help if his help was needed.

Rimma has a walking frame so Hussein walks slowly with her.

Liam has become more outgoing since he made friends with Peter.

Naseem and Usman are good friends but they don't enjoy the same novels.

**3** Replace the **adjectives** in brackets with more interesting adjectives.

We saw a (great) ____________ band called 'King Stingray' at a concert the other night. I loved their songs. They sing in Yolngu and English. They are (great) ____________ musicians.

I saw their music video 'Camp dog'. It was (great) ____________.

**4** Add one or more **clauses** to each sentence.

Bells work ______________________________________________

______________________________________________

Dog leashes work ______________________________________________

______________________________________________



*Grammar Rules! Student Book 3* (ISBN 9780655092438) © Tanya Gibb

**5** Complete each sentence with a **number adjective** from the box.

| |
|---|
| Some<br>Many<br>2<br>one<br>few |

Buy __________ litres of milk, please.

__________ people attended the concert.

__________ ducks swam on the lake.

A __________ houses were damaged in the storm.

Swallow __________ teaspoon of medicine.

**6** Underline the **noun groups**.

Our school won first prize in the music competition.

The town debating team won a few medals.

Most school excursions are enjoyable.

Thousands of people went to the music festival.

**7** Choose an **adverb** to begin each command.

| |
|---|
| Carefully<br>Gently<br>Clearly<br>Slowly |

______________ explain your invention.

______________ stir the mixture while it heats.

______________ collect the eggs.

______________ pat the puppies.

**8** Create **noun groups**. Add a word from each row to each noun below.

exciting healthy cute fresh ferocious

boxer male football orange breakfast

______________ ______________ game

______________ ______________ tiger

______________ ______________ puppy

______________ ______________ juice

______________ ______________ cereal

Unit 31

Collective nouns, pronouns, point of view

**1** Read *My Home.* Who do you think is telling the story in the poem?

______________________________________________________________________

**2** What is the **main idea** in the poem?

______________________________________________________________________

**3** Circle all the **pronouns** in the poem.

Who is *we, us, I*? ______________________________________________________________________

Who is *you*? ______________________________________________________________________

**4** Underline the **verbs** in the poem.

**5** What does this line tell you about the narrator's values? *where there was nothing but scrub.*

______________________________________________________________________

**6** What might *You* in the poem want to say to the person telling the story in the poem?

______________________________________________________________________



*Grammar Rules! Student Book 3* (ISBN 9780655092438) © Tanya Gibb

**Collective nouns** are names for groups of things. *bunch flock gang herd*
Collective nouns are singular.
*The flock has settled for the night.*

**7** Use a **collective noun** from the box to complete each **noun group**.

| pod | team |
|---|---|
| litter | herd |
| flock | school |

a ____________ of kittens a ____________ of whales
a ____________ of players a ____________ of cows
a ____________ of ducks a ____________ of fish

**8** Circle the correct **verb** or **verb group** in each row.

The herd ( is travelling / are travelling ) north.

The horses ( are galloping / is galloping ).

The pack of dingoes ( are monitored / is monitored ) by rangers.

The dingoes ( are / is ) hungry.

My mob ( are heading / is heading ) to town.

**9** Write a **personal pronoun** on each line to complete the sentences.

That seat is not yours. ____________ do not own ____________.

We live on Country. ____________ will look after ____________.

Listen to ____________. I will tell ____________ about Country.

The wild animals belong here. ____________ need to be protected.

Think about people in history who have had different **points of view**. Write a **poem** that shows the differences. Or, write a **poem** that shows one or more points of view about an issue in your home, community or school.

Unit 32

Types of sentences, point of view, antonyms

This text shows different **points of view**. It includes a variety of sentence types.

# Can We Negotiate?

'Pack up all your equipment, now,' requested Mum.

'Why can't we work on our project a bit longer?' whined Billy.

'I need the table for my work. Your experiment will have to wait until tomorrow,' insisted Mum.

'But Mum,' added Aggie, 'we just got everything organised. Can we just have another half an hour, PLEASE?'

'No! There's no time. I think it's a great project but it can wait. Finish it tomorrow,' declared Mum.

1. Read *Can We Negotiate?*. Highlight what Billy says in blue. Highlight what Mum says in red. Choose a different colour and highlight what Aggie says.

2. Circle the **saying verbs** in *Can We Negotiate?*.

3. Why do you think Mum is smiling in the illustration?

______________________________________________

4. Choose one **command** from *Can We Negotiate?*. Write it on the line.

______________________________________________

5. What does *negotiate* mean? Write a definition. Use a dictionary.

______________________________________________

6. What idea do the three people agree on in *Can We Negotiate?*?

______________________________________________



*Grammar Rules! Student Book 3* (ISBN 9780655092438) © Tanya Gibb

**7** Write a sentence of your own on each line. Use correct punctuation marks.

**Statement** ______________________

**Question** ______________________

**Command** ______________________

**Exclamation** ______________________

**8** Rewrite each sentence with correct punctuation.

thats unnecessary exclaimed reema ______________________

where is my hat questioned karl ______________________

i love lasagne stated fema ______________________

stop shouted the coach ______________________

**Rule**

**Antonyms** are words that have opposite meanings. Antonyms can often be formed using **prefixes** or **suffixes**.

*difficult/easy* *regular/irregular* *hopeful/hopeless*

**9** Write four **antonyms** for *great* as it is used in *Can We Negotiate?*.

______________________

**10** Write three **synonyms** that could be used instead of *whined* in *Can We Negotiate?*.

______________________

**11** Write three **synonyms** that could be used instead of *declared* in *Can We Negotiate?*.

______________________

**12** Sometimes the word *said* is used too often in texts. This can make the text sound boring. What other words could you use in your writing instead of *said*? Start a list of **synonyms** here.

______________________

Write a **discussion** between two or three people. Show that they have different opinions. Use punctuation marks and include statements, questions, commands and exclamations.

Unit 33

Pronouns, modal verbs, abstract nouns

This text is **informative**. It uses dot points and subheadings.

# Clever Inventions

First Nations Australians are clever inventors. Two of their cleverest inventions are:

- **Boomerangs**

Boomerangs were invented thousands of years ago. They were used for hunting and killing animals, in warfare or as digging sticks to dig vegetables from the ground. A boomerang could kill a kangaroo or emu 60m away from a thrower. Most boomerangs were non-returning. This clever invention is an important symbol of Australia.

- **Cultural burning**

Cultural burning is a method of controlled burning that First Nations Australians have used for thousands of years. Controlled burning is used to clear vegetation to make hunting easier, to encourage new plant growth and to prevent wildfires.

**1** Read *Clever Inventions*. List three uses for a boomerang.

______________________________

______________________________

______________________________

**2** What opinion does the writer of *Clever Inventions* have about boomerangs?

______________________________

**3** List three reasons for cultural burning.

______________________________

______________________________

______________________________



*Grammar Rules! Student Book 3* (ISBN 9780655092438) © Tanya Gibb

**4** Find and circle the **noun group** *This clever invention* in *Clever Inventions.*

What is *This clever invention?* ______________________________

**5** Circle the **modal verb** in the sentence that tells you that the result was not certain.

*A boomerang could kill a kangaroo or emu 60m away from a thrower.*

**6** Write a **personal pronoun** on each line.

Boomerangs were invented thousands of years ago. ________ were used for hunting.

The boomerang is a symbol of Australia. ________ is recognised internationally.

Cultural burning is a controlled burning. First Nations Australians have practised ________ for thousands of years.

**7** Write two **abstract nouns** used in *Clever Inventions.*

__________________ __________________

**Tip** Remember the rule on page 51.

**8** Tick the **sentence** that expresses the most certainty.

☐ Cultural burning might not prevent wildfires.

☐ Cultural burning will prevent wildfires.

☐ Cultural burning could help to prevent wildfires.

**9** Rewrite the sentences using correct **punctuation**.

boomerangs were invented in australia declared zali

______________________________

did you know that there are paintings of boomerangs on 20 000 year old rock art asked kyra

______________________________

______________________________

Research an Australian First Nations invention, such as the woomera, the didgeridoo or the waterbag. Create a **report** to present your research to your class or another group.

Unit 34

Personal pronouns, commas in lists, homophones, homonyms

This **information report** uses **personal pronouns** to refer to people and things and to make the text **cohesive**.

# The Invention of Money

It is thought that the Greeks invented the first money over two and a half thousand years ago. They made coins out of a mixture of gold and silver.

Before the invention of money, people traded items of value. For example, a farmer might trade a cow for two pigs. Other items that people traded were rice, tobacco, animal furs, whale teeth and gold.

Gold was a popular trading item, but it was too heavy to carry around, so people wrote promises on pieces of paper saying they would pay in gold. The first true paper money was probably invented in China.

**1** List the items people traded before the invention of money.

______________________________________________

**2** Circle a **sentence** in *The Invention of Money* that tells you the writer is not certain of the facts.

**3** Find a **personal pronoun** in *The Invention of Money*. ____________________

Who or what does the **pronoun** refer to? ____________________

**4** Write five **noun groups** used in *The Invention of Money*.

______________________________________________

Remember the rule on page 59.

**5** Write two **proper nouns** for people or countries used in *The Invention of Money*.

______________________________________________

**6** What was the advantage of paper money?

______________________________________________



*Grammar Rules! Student Book 3* (ISBN 9780655092438) © Tanya Gibb

**Commas** are used to separate items in a list of **nouns**. The word *and* is usually used instead of a comma between the last two items.
*rice, tobacco, animal furs, whale teeth and gold*

**7** Write lists. Use **commas** between each item and the word *and* between the last two items.

girls' names ____________, ____________, ____________ and ______________

boys' names ________________________________________________________________

friends' names ______________________________________________________________

items you could trade _________________________________________________________

____________________________________________________________________________

**Homophones** are words that sound the same but are spelled differently and mean different things. *flour* and *flower*
**Homonyms** sound the same and are spelled the same, but their meaning depends on the context. *A* *__bat__* *is a mammal. Get the cricket* *__bat__*.

**8** Find a **homophone** for *two* and *to* in *The Invention of Money*. ____________

**9** Circle the correct **homophone** in each sentence.

The ( sail / sale ) of the boat fluttered in the breeze.

The ( weather / whether ) was very mild.

( There / Their ) sailboat was very slow.

( Buy / By ) the time the wind picked up, we had to go home.

I ran out of ( flour / flower ) to make the cake.

**10** Circle the correct answer.

Dad asked two children, 'Who broke the vase?' He then said, 'Don't lie.'

He meant: a) Don't lie down. b) Don't tell untruths

Do some research on a topic of your choice. Write an **information report**. Use **personal pronouns** to refer to people or things you are writing about. Be careful not to give your opinions. Only write the facts.

# Unit 35 Revision

**1** Write a **sentence** that shows events happened in the **past**.

______________________________

**2** Write a **sentence** that shows events are happening now (**present tense**).

______________________________

**3** Write a **sentence** that shows events might happen in the **future**.

______________________________

**4** Write a **synonym** for each word.

awful ____________ scary ____________ huge ____________ amazing ____________

**5** Underline the **personal pronouns**.

I will discover the cure.

What are they testing in the laboratory?

She is a famous inventor.

Give the test results to him.

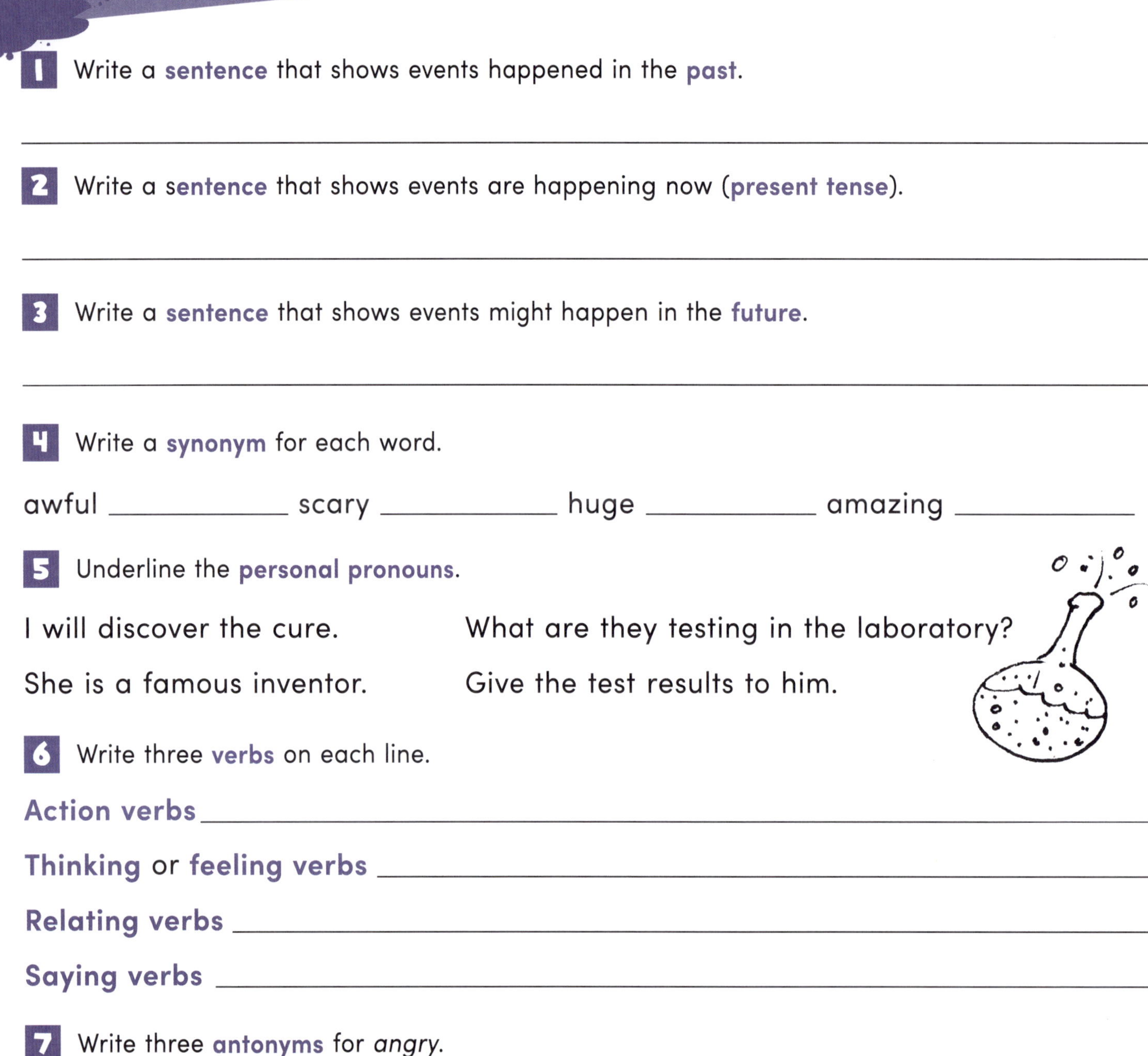

**6** Write three **verbs** on each line.

**Action verbs** ______________________________

**Thinking** or **feeling verbs** ______________________________

**Relating verbs** ______________________________

**Saying verbs** ______________________________

**7** Write three **antonyms** for *angry*.

____________ ____________ ____________

**8** Underline each statement that presents an opinion.

My cousin is greedy.

That's a funny movie.

The strawberries are expensive.

Chantel has black hair.

**9** Add **commas** to this sentence.

We will need a hammer some nails a piece of paper a pen and our thinking caps!



*Grammar Rules! Student Book 3* (ISBN 9780655092438) © Tanya Gibb

**10** Add punctuation to these sentences.

thats my hat shouted Raphael

does anyone have the football asked Jordan

come here commanded the teacher

we need to finish our group project today reminded Sunita

**11** Add **adjectives** to build interesting **noun groups** for a spooky story.

____________ ____________ wolf   ____________ ____________ castle

____________ ____________ forest   ____________ ____________ goblin

**12** Circle the correct **verb** or **verb group** in each row.

Mum ( goes / go ) to work by bus.

The herd of elephants ( are / is ) wary.

The team ( are heading / is heading ) to the oval.

Those dingoes ( are / is ) hungry.

**13** Add a **prefix** to each word to create **antonyms**.

understood ________________   responsible ________________

logical ________________   ability ________________

**14** Add a **conjunction** from the box to each sentence to join the clauses. Use a capital letter if the conjunction begins a sentence.

| although | unless | so | after |
|---|---|---|---|

Jasmine was scared of the dark ______________ she made her sister walk with her.

Lloyd couldn't watch television ______________ his homework was completed.

______________ his homework was completed, Lloyd watched television.

______________ Nikita wanted to watch her show, she let Gabby watch the news.

**15** Circle the **abstract nouns**.

footpath   idea   concrete   heavy   lonely   cleanliness

peace   education   history   pride   handshake   computer

# GLOSSARY

*Look at the page number in the circle to find more information about the rule or tip.*

**adjective**............a word that tells more about a **noun** 10

*to classify* 64

*to compare or show preference* 41

*to describe* 10 15

*to show possession* 59

*to tell number or quantity* 15 59

**adverb**................a word that modifies a **verb**, an **adjective** or another adverb to tell where, when or how

*where* 20 *how* 29

*when* 25 *modal adverbs* 35

**adverbial**...........a word, phrase or clause that tells where, when or how 20

**antonym**............a word that means the opposite of another word 71

**apostrophe**.......a punctuation mark; used in a **contraction** 23

*used to show possession* 23

**article**.................*(a, an, the)* used in front of a **noun** or at the beginning of a **noun group** 15

**body language**...........gestures and facial expressions used for effect and to influence listeners or viewers 34

**clause**.................a unit of meaning that includes a **verb** 11

*independent clause* 11 26

**comma**...............a punctuation mark that separates items in a series 37

*lists* 37 75 *used in quoted speech* 37

**command**..........a sentence that tells someone to do something 39

**conjunction**.......a type of connecting word that joins **clauses** in sentences 26 56

*coordinating conjunction* 26 56 *subordinating conjunction* 56

**connective**.........a word or words that link ideas through a text 46

**contraction**.......a word made by shortening words and leaving letters out 23

**emotive words**.words chosen to make readers or listeners feel a certain way 38 50

**evaluative word**...................words that tell us someone's opinion and judgement about something 33

**exclamation**......a word or sentence that shows strong emotion, or gives a warning or command; ends in an exclamation mark 28

**fact**.....................objective language; something that is usually accepted as true 47

**homonyms**.........words that sound the same and have the same spelling, so require context for meaning 75

**homophone**.......a word that sounds the same as another word but is spelled differently and means something different 75



*Grammar Rules! Student Book 3* (ISBN 9780655092438) © Tanya Gibb

**idiom**.................an expression that means something different from the words used 45

**imagery**............words that help create a picture in the mind or that appeal to the senses 44

**main idea**.........the idea the writer or speaker wants you to know or accept as true 22

**narrative voice**.the voice of the person telling the story (a first- or third-person narrator) 53

**noun**..................a naming word for people, places, animals and things, including ideas

*abstract* 51 *classifying* 64 *collective* 69

*common or proper* 8 *noun group* 15 59 *singular and plural* 27

**onomatopoeia**..when a word imitates a sound 29

**opinion**..............subjective language; a statement that reveals what the speaker or writer thinks 47

**personal pronoun**............a word that refers to or replaces a **noun** 12

**possessive pronoun**............a pronoun that shows possession 36

**prefix**.................letters or a word part added to the beginning of a word 59

**prepositional phrase**...............a group of words not including a verb and beginning with a preposition; can tell where, when or how 20

**question**............a sentence that asks for information or an opinion. It ends in a question mark. 24

**quoted speech**..the actual speech someone says; uses quotation marks 32

**sentence**............a group of words that makes sense on its own and includes at least one verb 11

*a simple sentence is one clause (includes one verb/verb group)* 11

*complex* 56 *a compound sentence contains two independent clauses joined by a coordinating conjunction* 26

**simile**................when something is said to be like or as something else 45

**statements**........a sentence that gives information or an opinion 24 47

**stereotype**.........a caricature or oversimplification of a person or thing 49

**subject-verb agreement**........the way the form of the verb changes to agree with its subject in number 27

**suffix**..................letters added to the end of words for plurals or to change word meanings 59

**synonym**............a word that has a similar meaning to another word 51

**tense**..................how the form of the **verb** changes to anchor events in time (past, present, future) 9 52

**verb**....................a word that tells what is happening in a **clause**

*action* 9 *modal* 35 57 *relating (being)* 25 *saying* 16

*tense* 9 52 *thinking and feeling* 13 *verb group* 63

**voice**..................the volume, pace and tone of speech used for effect 34

*Grammar Rules! Student Book 3* (ISBN 9780655092438) © Tanya Gibb

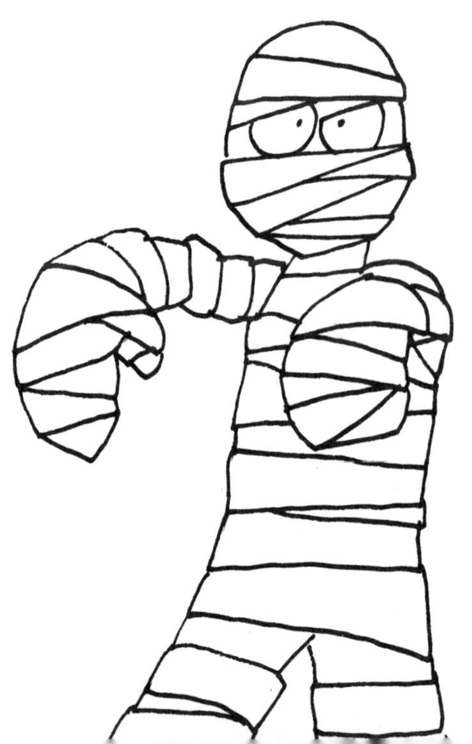